Cambridge Elements ≡

Elements in World Englishes
edited by
Edgar W. Schneider
University of Regensburg

TRANSNATIONAL KOREAN ENGLISHES

Sofia Rüdiger
University of Bayreuth

Alex Baratta
University of Manchester

CAMBRIDGE
UNIVERSITY PRESS

CAMBRIDGE
UNIVERSITY PRESS

Shaftesbury Road, Cambridge CB2 8EA, United Kingdom

One Liberty Plaza, 20th Floor, New York, NY 10006, USA

477 Williamstown Road, Port Melbourne, VIC 3207, Australia

314–321, 3rd Floor, Plot 3, Splendor Forum, Jasola District Centre,
New Delhi – 110025, India

103 Penang Road, #05–06/07, Visioncrest Commercial, Singapore 238467

Cambridge University Press is part of Cambridge University Press & Assessment,
a department of the University of Cambridge.

We share the University's mission to contribute to society through the pursuit of
education, learning and research at the highest international levels of excellence.

www.cambridge.org
Information on this title: www.cambridge.org/9781009519342

DOI: 10.1017/9781009519366

When citing this work, please include a reference to the DOI 10.1017/9781009519366

First published 2025

A catalogue record for this publication is available from the British Library

ISBN 978-1-009-51934-2 Hardback
ISBN 978-1-009-51931-1 Paperback
ISSN 2633-3309 (online)
ISSN 2633-3295 (print)

Transnational Korean Englishes

Elements in World Englishes

DOI: 10.1017/9781009519366
First published online: January 2025

Sofia Rüdiger
University of Bayreuth

Alex Baratta
University of Manchester

Author for correspondence: Sofia Rüdiger, sofia.ruediger@uni-bayreuth.de

Abstract: *Transnational Korean Englishes* presents the many faces of English in South Korea (henceforth also Korea) – from Korean English forms and functions to English loanwords in Korean, and from the influences of Korean on the English language to Korean cultural exports. Drawing on specialized and purpose-built spoken and written corpora and other empirical data as well as previous studies, the Element illuminates the Korean-English language contact setting from a range of perspectives, shining light on various transnational Korean English phenomena. Guided by questions of legitimization and codification, this Element shows Koreans as productive and creative users of localized English forms, with hallyu (the Korean Wave) promoting not only Korean pop cultural products around the world but also contributing to influences of Korean on English worldwide.

Keywords: World Englishes, Korean English, Konglish, K-pop, Hallyu

ISBNs: 9781009519342 (HB), 9781009519311 (PB), 9781009519366 (OC)
ISSNs: 2633-3309 (online), 2633-3295 (print)

Contents

1 South Korea: From Hermit Kingdom to Global Player

Introduction

The Republic of Korea (referred to hereafter as 'Korea' or 'South Korea') has changed in many ways since the end of the Korean War in 1953[1] – which is a good starting point for the discussion that follows, as it helps to illustrate just how far Korea has come. In 1953, Korea was one of the poorest countries in the world – it relied on foreign aid, most people lived in poverty, and few were literate (Miley, 2023). Contrast that with the 1980s, when Korea had advanced to a middle-income country, having experienced rapid industrialization and being known as one of the 'Asian Tigers' (next to Hong Kong, Singapore, and Taiwan). It is clearly the case that Korea has become a thriving, modern, and vibrant country, well known for its food, film production and, of course, its music and TV dramas. Some of Korea's cultural exports have been seen and heard on a global scale, such as the 2012 hit song *Gangnam Style* by Psy as well as the 2019 Academy Award winning film *Parasite*. At the time of writing, K-pop sensation BTS had won twelve Billboard Music Awards and earned twenty-six Guinness World Records (including most Twitter engagements; see BBC, 2018). It is perhaps unsurprising, then, that Korean language courses are more common now than ever before, with the Korea Foundation revealing that the number of global institutions offering Korean studies increased to over 1,300 in the decade following 2007 (see Korea Foundation, n.d.). And beyond Korea's cultural exports, we should also consider its technological exports of items like cars, refrigerators, and phones, recognized with respective – and trusted – brands, such as Hyundai, LG, and Samsung. While Korean culture, from food to language, is widely recognized, one aspect is still less well understood: The ways in which Koreans have made the English language their own and how Korean Englishes have become a transnational phenomenon. This is what this Element seeks to address, and in doing so we will focus on the following key points:

- The Korean–English language contact setting and its outcomes are complex and dynamic;
- *Korean English* and *Korean Englishes* are more fitting terms to use as opposed to *English in Korea* and *Konglish*; following Lee and Jenks (2017), we use the plural form *Korean Englishes* to acknowledge the exist-ence of subvariation but also draw on the singular *Korean English* as an

---

[1] Technically, the war did not end, as there was no peace treaty signed, but an armistice has been in effect for more than seventy years.

umbrella term (akin to nomenclature in World Englishes research – cf. *Singapore English, American English, South African English*);

- While *Konglish* is a term largely used to refer to, as we do here, a lexical set (comprising a subset of English words used in Korea; see Section 3), Korean English goes beyond lexis and incorporates grammatical innovations – this in turn points to the nativization of a language variety;
- Korean English is not 'bad' English or a failed attempt to master the English language; thus, we are approaching Korean English as an English variety in its own right;
- There are numerous transnational aspects to consider, moving, for instance, from English words being used in Korea to Korean words taking prominence outside of Korea; indeed, Korean words are used by non-Koreans on a wide scale.

Before we present an overview of previous linguistic research on the forms and the variety status of Korean English, we first consider the origins of English in Korea, to better understand the journey it has taken from the end of the Korean War to the present day, including contemporary functions across society and language attitudes.

Historical Development of English in Korea

As mentioned, after the Korean War, Korea was economically devastated. What followed, however, was a period of rapid economic growth, dubbed the *Miracle on the Han River* (i.e., the river that runs through the Korean capital, Seoul). Government policies were of course a large part of this, involving the expansion of agriculture and energy industries, such as electronics, as well as the development of roads and railways. Moreover, the beginning of a global recognition of Korea was certainly helped by its hosting of the 1988 (Summer) Olympics, as well as co-hosting the 2002 World Cup and, most recently, the Korean Winter Olympics in 2018. Combined, we see a country that is recognized for its economic strength, technological development, and modernization, in addition to its involvement in international events, here sports. Throughout this period, from 1953 onwards, English has been establishing its presence in Korea, alongside more obvious developments tied to the economy and politics, changing the country from the so-called *hermit kingdom* to a well-established and modern nation (see Rüdiger, in press, for a more detailed overview of these historical developments in relation to English).

The first English school opened in Korea in 1883 (Nahm, 1993); however, English in Korea only gained a solid foothold with the stationing of US soldiers following the Korean War, with a sizeable US military presence still in Korea to this day. In fact, after World War II, South Korea was briefly under US Army rule, namely, from 1950 to 1953. This period is referred to as *United States Army Military Government in Korea* (USAMGIK) and, importantly, this military government reinstated English education in Korean schools (which had been abolished during the Japanese occupation of Korea from 1910 to 1945) (see Kim, 2011), while also operating under English as its official language (Kim, 2015). It is for these historical and political reasons that American English is the clear target variety in Korean English language education.

In the meantime, English has become firmly entrenched in the Korean education system and, since 1997, it has been a mandatory subject from 3rd grade elementary school onwards (Jung & Norton, 2002: 247), with many Korean children starting voluntary English education even earlier, via kindergarten classes and private language education. English plays a central role in Korea's university entrance exam, *suneung*, and is often essential for job attainment and promotion (independent of actual use at work). Despite the lack of home acquisition of English and even though

> Korea was never colonized by an English-speaking country, the strong military presence and economic and cultural influence of the United States in the southern half of the Korean peninsula that continue to the present day make Korea comparable in important ways to former colonies of English-speaking nations. (Park, J. S.-Y., 2009: 18)

It is nevertheless difficult to find accurate statistics on how many South Korean people use English – and with which level of proficiency they do so. Education First's English Proficiency Index (EPI) ranks South Korea number five in Asia, surpassed only by regional settings with an (English) postcolonial background, namely, Singapore, the Philippines, Malaysia, and Hong Kong (Education First, n.d.). In order to fully grasp the role English plays in present-day Korean society, we next examine its functional range in more detail.

Functions of English in the South Korean Context

The most obvious function of English in South Korea is as a lingua franca between Koreans and foreigners – not only in tourism and business contexts but also in many academic settings. We already mentioned the importance of English in the Korean education system, but there is indeed a bit more to it than meets the eye. The possibility to engage in educational activities related to English in Korea are endless, from 'English villages,' which emulate life in a nonspecified 'English' town (Lee, 2011a) to the many summer and winter schools, often referred to as *English camps*, as well as the countless private institutes all over Korea, known as *hagwon*, which provide additional academic tuition in various subjects beyond regular school, of which English is one of the most common. Institutions like the Korean Minjok Leadership Academy (KMLA) adopt English-only policies, with students expected to use English all day in class, from Monday to Saturday (Lee, 2020). Many Korean universities offer English-only classes (see Kang, 2012) as a means to contribute to internationalization strategies and to incorporate increasing numbers of foreign students, a move that has also been received critically (see, e.g., Cho, 2012). English use on campus is not restricted to classroom activities: Thorkleson (2005), for instance, examined the use of English in student news articles written by Korean university students and Baratta (2021) reported on English clubs, which abound on Korean university campuses.

In the workplace, English usage is highly dependent on the context – for instance, depending on whether communication with foreign customers is necessary. We also do not want to downplay the role other languages, such as Japanese and Chinese, play in the Korean context. Nevertheless, it is English proficiency that is seen as crucial for job opportunities and for securing a high-value job in many cases in the first place. This in turn also rests to a high degree on university placement, which again depends on performance in *suneung* – the Korean university placement test (officially also known as the College Scholastic Ability Test or CSAT), in which English is one of six subjects. Taking this into consideration it might not be surprising that Koreans spend record amounts on private education in general (Park & Kang, 2024), with the largest share of this going to English education: On average, Korean households spend 248,000 won (more than $US 180) per month for private English education (Park & Kang, 2024). Not coincidentally then, the desire for English in Korea has been described as a sickness (cf. the notion of 'English Fever'; see Park, J.-K., 2009), with some Korean mothers taking their children overseas to countries, such as the USA, Canada, or Singapore, so that their children can be immersed in an English-language setting temporarily, often while the fathers provide financial assistance from Korea. This phenomenon is referred to as *gireogi appa* (기러기 아빠, 'wild goose dad'),[2] a reference to wild geese and migration (cf. Lee, S. H., 2019, 2021).

However, there are also many other domains of English use across the country – outside of educational settings – and someone arriving in Korea for the first time might indeed be surprised at the wealth of English that can be encountered (amply documented by research; see the cited literature for only some examples). As one of Jamie Shinhee Lee's elderly Korean study

---

[2] Throughout the manuscript, we use the Revised Romanization system for Korean (without indication of syllable boundaries).

participants exclaimed: "Everywhere you go, you see English!" (Lee, 2016). This includes national English-language newspapers, for example, *The Korea Times* and *The Korea Herald* (Jung & Min, 1999); code-switching to English on many TV dramas (Baratta, 2014), reality TV (Lee, 2013), and in TV commercials (Lee, 2006); English used extensively as part of public signage and on shop fronts (Lawrence, 2012; Tan & Tan, 2015); English–Korean code-mixing in K-pop (Jin & Ryoo, 2014; Rüdiger, 2021a); and, of course, the many Koreans who use English in daily life (Lee, 2016; Baratta, 2021), though admittedly the language of choice between Koreans in private communication, barring special circumstances, is usually Korean.

Beyond its ubiquity in K-pop, which has been described as "the public discursive space in which English use is most prevalent" (Lee, 2004: 433; see also Section 5), English is also present in other media and pop culture products, such as movies and television, where it has been shown to have different functions. For instance, code-switching between Korean and English in Korean TV shows can be used to index a modern identity (see Baratta, 2014), while at the same time also contributing to a language ideology of self-deprecation (Park, J. S.-Y., 2009) by depicting Koreans (or specific groups of Koreans, such as the elderly) as having low English proficiencies (Park, 2003; Lee, 2014).

Korean cinemas generally do not dub their movies and English-language productions (except for children's movies) are thus usually shown in the original version (with subtitles). One must keep in mind, however, that Korea has a strong local film industry, and in 2023, for instance, of the top 20 most watched movies only eight were US/English-language productions (Korean Film Council, n.d.). Nevertheless, this translates into a considerable market share of English-language movies, providing further points of contact for spoken English in Korea. Last but not least, we can mention here how Korean movie productions have also registered 'English' as a topic of filmographic concern. A prime example can be found in the Korean movie "Please Teach Me English" (original title: 영어완전정복; *Yeongeo Wanjeon Jeongbok*) from 2004, which packages the notion of 'English Fever' in South Korea into a comic love story. Lee (2012: 129) has found that the movie indeed presents a "realistic portrayal of a wide range of emotions that are often believed to be evoked by the English language: fear, desperation and frustration, along with a sense of achievement and empowerment."

Considering Korean advertising, we can identify a great deal of English usage, seen for example in slogans, such as "Excellence in Flight" (Korean Air), "Life's Good" (LG), and "Do What You Can't" (Samsung). Lee (2006) points to the creativity and word play involved with the language of advertising and reminds us once again that English as used in Korea is indeed sometimes primarily for domestic consumption, seen for example in a commercial for a *moving bra* (a local English form for *push-up bra*). Going beyond advertising, researchers such as Tan and Tan (2015) and Lawrence (2012) have examined the linguistic landscape in Korea and found abundant usage of English on (mainly unofficial) signage (e.g., in shop windows). Last but not least, we want to turn to the digital realm. While the internet is a multilingual space, it might be no surprise that, globally, English takes the largest share according to traffic analysis: 52.1 percent of web content is in English, with Korean content making up 0.8 percent (numbers from January 2024; Petrosyan, 2024). No doubt, Koreans do use and produce online content in Korean (e.g., on the Korean-exclusive online platform *Naver*), but certainly the internet in general and social media specifically provide manifold opportunities to engage with English(es) (see also Rüdiger, Leuckert & Leimgruber, in press). Nevertheless, research on Koreans' online media consumption and production involving Englishes is scarce. In general, it is not difficult to find Korean English usage online though and as an illustrative example we provide a short look at Korean real estate websites.[3]

Numerous real estate websites catering specifically to the Korean context are targeted at expats and thus operate in English. Looking for housing on sites such as *Seoul Homes*[4] or *Seoul Houses*[5] confronts English-speaking expats with a number of localized words related to the semantic field of housing. Among the housing types offered on *Seoul Homes* one finds, for instance, *officetels* (e.g., "Large lofty type officetel near Gangnam Stn. short term available").[6] Other residential types referenced are *villas* and *hanok houses*. Clicking on an ad on *Seoul Homes* one might be informed that "discuss required." Likewise, short-term visitors to Korea looking for accommodation on local English-language sites like *Goshipages*[7] will find *goshiwon* and *livingtels* as potential options for shorter stays. While these terms are widely known to Koreans and expatriates residing in Korea and are amply documented in local English usage, others might have to resort to web searches to find out more. There are doubtlessly more arenas where English plays

---

[3] Korean real estate websites make an excellent starting point for a short case study due to their geographical tie to the South Korean geographical context.

[4] https://seoulhomes.kr/.   [5] http://seoulhouses.co.kr/.

[6] We provide here the definitions for the accommodation types mentioned in the text:
- *officetel*: a blend of *office* and *hotel*; a building that serves as both one's residence and place of business
- *villa*: a multi-unit residential building with a low number of floors (*not* a luxurious accommodation)
- *hanok house*: a traditional Korean house
- *goshiwon*: furnished, very small single room (usually for students)
- *livingtel*: a blend of *living* and *hotel*; a long-term hotel-style accommodation

[7] https://goshipages.com/.

an important role in Koreans' online life, some but not all of them related to communication with foreigners (as the one we just presented) – the detailed study of these remains an important desideratum for future research. Next, we present a short survey of language attitudes toward English in the Korean setting.

Attitudes Toward English in Korea

Public attitudes toward a particular variety of English, or other languages copresent with English in a specific setting, are an important aspect in World Englishes research. In the context of English in Korea, we have already mentioned the notion of 'English Fever,' which stands for the extreme desire 'for English' per se. The list of phenomena pertinent to English Fever in South Korea spans, among others, 'linguistic' (tongue) surgery for Korean children (a frenectomy), the aforementioned 'wild geese parenting' situations to enable early childhood study abroad, and the exceptionally high expenses dedicated to private English education in its various guises (see also Park, J.-K., 2009). It is no surprise then that attitudes toward English are not only positive. Joseph Sung-Yul Park (2009) aptly summarized three prevailing, partially contradicting, language ideologies of English that can be found in South Korean society at large: (1) Externalization (English as a language of the 'Other,' i.e., non-Korean), (2) self-deprecation (Koreans as unable to use English proficiently), and (3) necessitation (English proficiency as a necessary skill in today's glo-balized world). As this shows, language attitudes in Korea are by all means complex (and surprisingly underresearched, taking aside studies working with language professionals, such as teachers and translators; see Cho, 2017). Due to its connection to expensive private English education and other educational opportunities, English has been described as a "class marker" in Korean society (Park & Abelmann, 2004: 646) and is considered essential for upward social mobility. Park and Abelmann (2004: 666) described how there exist three 'meanings' of English in Korea, with English being seen as

(1) providing local opportunities (e.g., in school, university, and work)
(2) providing opportunities abroad (e.g., working abroad)
(3) "satisfy[ing] cosmopolitan strivings" (i.e., preservation and/or ascendency of social class).

This connection between English and socioeconomic status and opportunities has consistently been made by numerous researchers and persists to the present day (cf. Park, 2013; Choi, L., 2021; Lee, C., 2021).

Returning to educational contexts in general and to Korean English(es) specifically, Ahn (2014: 196) points out that attitudes toward languages "are subject to change according to socio [*sic*], political and economic power shifts." While Ahn's study involving Korean and non-Korean English as a Foreign Language (EFL) teachers did involve a degree of reported confusion regarding what Korean English is and the belief that it is not a 'real' English, there were indeed positive responses. For example, some teachers explained that Korean English has "strong features" and "effectively expressed Korean culture" (Ahn, 2014: 214). This can potentially be related to the fact that a number of teacher education programs in Korea regard American English as only one example of the many Englishes (and cultures) that are used in the world, and not the sole variety to be propagated (Kang, 2017). There are many TESOL (Teaching English to Speakers of Other Languages) programs that feature World Englishes as part of the curriculum, thus avoiding the hegemonic grip that Inner Circle varieties have otherwise enjoyed. Language is a cultural conduit and thus, given the Korean cultural wave (see Section 5), the respect, even admiration, for Korean culture might extend to its variety of English too. While it is certainly the case that many Koreans, teachers and parents in particular, regard Inner Circle standards as the only legitimate variety of English, given its use in academic testing, it is probable that parts of the younger Korean generation, and certainly many global K-fans, regard Korean English wholly positively. There is evidence for such positivity in a study by Baratta (2019), in which a young Korean man admonished attitudes that regard Korean English as not being 'pure,' citing all manner of linguistic influence on English in the first instance. Clearly, more research is needed to gather the current attitudes toward Korean English, gleaned from Koreans from all walks of life. Another research desideratum lies in a large-scale acceptability study of Korean English features, for instance, those pointed out in the next section.

Conclusion

Having thus covered a first introduction to Korea and its variety of English, the Element now continues with a focus on the forms and variety status of Korean English, focusing mainly on morpho-syntactic features. In Section 3, we turn to English loanwords in Korean and a term that is often used to refer to them, that is, *Konglish*. Drawing on large-scale corpus evidence, Section 4 expands on the opposite case, namely, Korean words used by English speakers around the world. Last but not least, Section 5 comes to truly transnational phenomena related to (pop) culture, such as K-pop, mukbang, and food.

2 Korean English: Forms and Variety Status

Introduction

In this section, we survey the existing research on the forms of Korean English and the implications for variety status. We focus specifically on selected corpus-based or data-centered studies of written and spoken Korean English, which have pointed out several potentially nativized or nativizing forms (e.g., Shim, 1999; Hadikin, 2014; Rüdiger, 2019, 2021a; Leuckert & Rüdiger, 2020). Where relevant, we provide (yet unpublished) examples for features and patterns from the Spoken Korean English Corpus (SPOKE; Rüdiger, 2016). We additionally draw on case studies from the Korean linguistic landscape and academic writing to further enrich our overview. We close this section with a brief discussion of the implications of research on the forms of Korean English for variety status and World Englishes modeling.

Written Forms of Korean English

We begin our overview with a look at written forms and in particular those found in educational material, namely, a school-based textbook, and Korean English newspapers. The former is based on the groundbreaking work by Shim (1999), who published one of the first empirical studies on Korean English. In her article, Shim examined forms of English in Korea using *High School English I: Teacher's Guide* (Chang et al., 1989), which was in use from 1987 to 1995. According to Shim (1999: 250), the guide represents "the final product of the past 50 years of the codification of Korean English," and is of particular relevance to us here as it (1) represents a codified form of Korean English as found in an official textbook used in schools, but also (2) constitutes part of the teaching material encountered by Korean English speakers who went to high school during that timeframe. This includes many of the speakers from SPOKE, the spoken Korean English corpus, which we will introduce and draw on later.[8] A more recent look at English textbooks used in Korean (middle) schools can be found in Kim and Lee (2023), though their focus is on matters of identity representation and not Korean English forms as such. Another current turn of events that needs to be mentioned here is the development of a 'home-grown' English proficiency test, the Test of English Proficiency (TEPS), produced by Seoul National University.[9] This points to potential first steps in distancing from

---

[8] Note that it is not entirely clear which textbooks were used in the education of the SPOKE speakers, but based on the timeframe the textbook was used, it is likely that many of them were exposed to this, or similar, material.

[9] Cf. https://en.teps.or.kr/about_teps.html.

the so-far exonormative orientation in language testing, though US-based tests like TOEFL (Test of English as a Foreign Language) and TOEIC (Test of English for International Communication) are by far and large still the go-to option in the Korean setting (see Park, 2024).

The codified forms in the Korean English textbook attested by Shim (1999) range from lexico-semantics and pragmatics to morpho-syntax. We provide selected examples for the first two and then focus on morpho-syntax for the remainder of this section as this is the field that has received most attention in World Englishes research to date. Altogether the list of lexico-semantic Korean English forms spans eight items (all collected from the first chapter of the textbook alone) and includes items such as *on life* (used with the meaning of 'alive') and *day by day* (used with the meaning of 'daily') (Shim, 1999: 251–252). The use of *no wonder* in conversation-initial position (instead of as a rejoinder to what has been said before) – for instance in "No wonder you can't sleep well when you eat too much" (Shim, 1999: 251) – might for some already be counted as part of the realm of pragmatics. Here, Shim (1999: 254–255), briefly, refers to phenomena related to formality, negative tags, and politeness. The morpho-syntactic features listed by Shim (1999: 252–254) are quite comprehensive and involve, among others, definite articles (i.e., non-differentiation between definite and indefinite articles, with a definite article being used as the default form when the noun is postmodified by a prepositional phrase or a relative clause), noncount nouns used as count nouns, unidiomatic verb collocations (e.g., *talk together* instead of *talk with each other*), interchangeable uses of the present and the present progressive as well as simple past and past perfect, and the lack of a distinction between real and unreal conditions in conditional sentences.

The second seminal study we want to mention here is by Jung and Min (1999), who based their research on a corpus of 126 Korean English newspaper articles taken from *The Korea Herald*. They used this dataset to investigate selected modals and prepositions. In terms of frequency, they found that *will* is used with considerably higher frequency in the Korean English newspapers when compared to American English, British English, and Australian English data (53.6 vs. 27.0, 28.0, and 34.2 instances per 10,000 words; Jung & Min, 1999: 27). *Would* and *shall*, however, remain below the usage frequencies of the other varieties. Fine-grained semantic analysis revealed no clear differences in the meaning expressed with the modals (Jung & Min, 1999: 32–33), but in some cases the Korean English data patterned more closely with the American English data than the other varieties, which corresponds to the historically and politically conditioned status of American English as target and input variety in the Korean context (see Section 1). In terms of prepositions, Jung and Min (1999) focused on the spatial meanings of *in* and *at*. There they found instances of the two prepositions swapped with each other as in (1) and (2) (both examples from Jung & Min, 1999: 34).

(1) An earlier meeting **at** Cheju set the stage for a renewed peace effort.
(2) The writer is a visiting professor of linguistics **in** Korea University.

The authors give two possible explanations for this: Errors made by the editorial team or substrate language influence from Korean. Due to limitations in corpus size,[10] they were unable to come up with a conclusive explanation. Nevertheless, their research provides early indications for the potential development of Korean English forms, which was taken up by spoken language research.

Spoken Forms of Korean English

We focus here, mainly, on results obtained from the Spoken Korean English corpus (aka SPOKE), which was collected by the first author in 2014. The SPOKE corpus was designed to specifically elicit conversational and informal data, following the 'cuppa coffee approach' (see Rüdiger, 2016). The data collection captured the use of English by 115 Korean speakers (64 women and 51 men aged between 18 and 44 with an average of 27 years; 65 students, 42 employees, 4 students who also worked full time, and 4 unemployed persons) in 60 hours of recordings, subsequently orthographically transcribed to form the SPOKE corpus. Based on this corpus, Rüdiger (2019) provided a detailed first exploration of spoken Korean English morpho-syntax centered around five parts of speech: Nouns, pronouns, articles, prepositions, and verbs. While some of the investigated features turned out to be unproductive (e.g., countable use of non-count nouns), others potentially form part of an emerging Korean English repertoire. Specifically, Rüdiger (2019: 202) lists:

— reduced plural redundancy on nouns after quantifiers, numerals, and in cases of context-given plurality

(3) I have **many dream** (SPOKE_63m27)[11]

---

[10] Note that Jung and Min (1999) never give their corpus size in words; all we know is that the total corpus spans 126 articles. Limitation in corpus size, however, is specifically mentioned by Jung and Min (1999) as a drawback of their work.

[11] Corpus speakers are identified with a string starting with the corpus name (SPOKE), followed by speaker number, speaker gender (m = male; f = female), and speaker age. In this example, speaker #63 was a 27-year-old man.

(4) they had **two daughter** and they always had a party in their room (SPOKE_92f24)

(5) I like **movie** mh I like SF and action (SPOKE_76m29)

– minus-pronouns[12] (mainly *I* in subject position, *it* in subject position, and *it* in object position)

(6) Ø actually do lots of homeworks in major (SPOKE_61f21)

(7) yah for him Ø was very easy (SPOKE_47f30)

(8) it's really good and I I recommend Ø (SPOKE_33f26)

– nonconventional use of definite articles (plus- and minus-) with selected nouns and expressions

(9) when will you leave **the** Korea? (SPOKE_117m22)

(10) some of my close friends were like from (.) Ø United States and Australia (SPOKE_17f24)

– minus-indefinite articles with selected nouns and expressions

(11) I hope (laughs) uh go to Bali with within Ø few years I think (SPOKE_36m28)

– minus-prepositions (in particular after verbs of motion; most often concerning the preposition *to*)

(12) so like Easter holiday and Christmas holiday I could go Ø Italy and London (SPOKE_25f27)

– plus-prepositions as part of innovative prepositional verbs or in combination with adverbs

(13) it's very dark so that many babies are just falling **in** a sleep (SPOKE_3f29)

– minus-copular verbs (in particular when followed by adjectives)

(14) and coffee Ø also very cheap over there (SPOKE_44f27)

– minus-lexical verbs in the infinitive, at times due to innovative conversion processes

(15) many people can't **tennis** (SPOKE_76m29).

Subsequent work based on SPOKE has delved into information-structure and discourse-pragmatic features, with Leuckert and Rüdiger (2020), for instance, showing that topicalization frequencies in Korean English (see [16]) are similar to British and American English data, but left-dislocation (see [17]) is much more frequent – that is, four times as frequent as in American English data.

(16) lots of alcohol they have (SPOKE_94f28) (cf. *they have lots of alcohol*)

(17) so (2) with that money *my husband and me* **we** will enjoy our life (SPOKE_3f29)

---

[12] More information on the plus- and minus- terminology can be found in Rüdiger (2019: 47–48). In short, *minus-X* refers to a nonconventional nonuse of a feature and *plus-X* to a nonconventional use of a feature.

In addition, discourse-pragmatic *like* (see [18] and [19]) was established as part of the Korean English repertoire, including quotative use (see [20]) (Rüdiger, 2021b).

(18) so **like** after learning for a year I thought oh English literature is actually really fun (SPOKE_55f19)

(19) they don't generally play **like** alternative rock or I mean quite soft rock (SPOKE_51m26)

(20) **I was like** (.) do you know where Taiwan is? and **he was like** yah *taeguk*[13] (SPOKE_68f22)

This finding is particularly relevant as

> discourse markers and particles are outside of the scope of many classroom activities, maybe even more so in the test-driven language learning environment of South Korea ..., this is an important hint towards language contact outside of the classroom setting (such as via pop culture, media consumption, usage with English-speaking acquaintances and friends) and contradicts the conceptualization of Korean English as learner language. (Rüdiger, 2021b: 558)

Beyond SPOKE, other corpus-based work taking a World Englishes perspective on spoken Korean English is scarce. Hadikin's (2014) corpus-based study on collocations is a welcome exception. Specifically, Hadikin focused on three short lexical strings (*do you know, but you know,* and *and you know*) and showed how frequencies and usage patterns by the Korean English speakers differed from British English reference corpora to a degree which he takes as "evidence supporting the idea that Korean English is a variety in its own right" (Hadikin, 2014: 178). Specifically, his results show that Koreans (living either in South Korea or the UK) tend to use *but you know* far more than the British speakers, specifically with the function to buy "more time for online speech processing" (Hadikin, 2014: 76).

It is important to point out that features identified as part of nontraditional varieties of English (i.e., Outer and Expanding Circle Englishes) – and this includes the ones we mentioned in this section – are not necessarily used by all speakers and writers of said variety (Mesthrie & Bhatt, 2008), neither are they usually exclusive to a specific variety (which is aptly demonstrated in the *Electronic World Atlas of Varieties of English*, which shows the regional spread of specific features; see Kortmann, Lunkenheimer & Ehret, 2020). This suggests that the features presented thus far form part of a Korean English feature pool (cf. Mufwene, 2001; Percillier, 2016; Rüdiger, 2019), which can be drawn on depending on factors like context, individual speaker, setting, conversational

---

[13] *Taeguk* (태국) is the Korean word for 'Thailand.'

partner, and so on. While we cannot provide details of use for every feature that we presented, in the following, we want to consider one selected morpho-syntactic feature more closely, namely, plus-definite articles.

Case Study: Plus-Definite Articles in Korean English

We have singled out plus-definite articles in Korean English for our case study as it is a feature mentioned already in Shim's (1999) work on codified forms in an English textbook used in Korea. In addition, articles occur highly frequently across text types in English and are thus particularly suitable for this kind of case study approach (where we only look at a limited number of data points). We illustrate the use of plus-definite articles across three domains of use: Spoken Korean English, the linguistic landscape, and academic writing. These usage contexts present different modes (spoken vs. written), levels of formality (informal vs. formal), and publicity (private vs. public). While Korean has a range of determiners at its disposal (e.g., 저, *jeo*, 'that'), this does not include articles – neither definite nor indefinite.

Evidence from Spoken Language – Conversations

We begin our case study with a short look at plus-definite articles in spoken Korean English as found in previous research. Examples for this, from qualitative research, can be found in (21), which was termed an 'error' by Morrett (2011: 22), and (22), which was described as 'irregular' by Rüdiger (2014: 13).

(21) I don't know about *the basketball* (Morrett, 2011: 22)
(22) on *the Twitter* Britney Spears followed me (Rüdiger, 2014: 13)

Drawing on the SPOKE corpus, Rüdiger (2019: 116–131) considered (definite) article use in numerous selected contexts in detail and found, for example, that plus-definite articles with nouns denoting social institutions occurred in 8 percent of the cases. For quantifying expressions this was at 3 percent and for temporal expressions at 4 percent. For proper nouns, the rates were 5 percent for country names, 10 percent for continent names, 6 percent for other place names, and 3 percent for language names. There was also a total of 78 occurrences of plus-definite articles followed by a deverbal noun in *-ing* (e.g., "the body was *the exploding*"; Rüdiger, 2019: 130). According to these numbers, plus-definite articles are rather rare in spoken conversational Korean English when compared to zero uses. Nevertheless, the usage is clearly identifiable in the data. In addition,

Rüdiger (2019) only focused on article use in specific syntactic and semantic contexts or slots. We therefore selected six random files from SPOKE – three from female speakers and three from male speakers – and tagged them manually for the use of plus-definite articles. Altogether we were able to identify 17 plus-definite articles (in a total of 17,661 words of speech), and while the number is relatively small, all speakers in the sample used a plus-definite article at least once. Our analysis revealed a number of instances which would have been missed in Rüdiger (2019), such as (23) and (24), where the use of the plus-definite article indicates a specific reference even though generic reference would be expected.

(23) yeah I don't like *the salt* (Speaker3m)
(24) I think he had like two years off *the work* to like study or something (Speaker2f)

It might be interesting to extend this type of analysis to the SPOKE corpus as a whole to see if this reveals further patterns related to plus-definite article use in conversational settings. We next turn to more public forms of language use, namely, the linguistic landscape and academic writing.

Evidence from Written Language – Linguistic Landscape

Our first example of a plus-definite article from the linguistic landscape in Korea is provided in Figure 1. The picture was taken by the second author in July 2023, during a trip to Seoul, and was found on the subway.

For this kind of public signage, that identifies a seat which is reserved for pregnant women, one might expect to find a construction such as 'seat for pregnant women.' In Figure 1, however, we see the use of a singular noun in combination with a definite article ("seat for *the pregnant woman*").[14] While the use of a plus-definite article could be interpreted as a form of hypercorrection, it can also be claimed that the definite article serves communicative functions, such as adding emphasis and to draw further attention to the recipient of the focus – here, the pregnant woman who is the intended user of the reserved subway seat.

The next sign we want to present was displayed at Lotte World, an amusement park in Korea. The sign in question can be found as a photograph on an online blog (Story of Mandy, 2010). It shows the bilingual logo of "Kiddie Land" and is titled "Stroller Custody"[15] (both in English and Korean). It then

---

[14] Note that the Korean original version in this bilingual sign (and also the following one) does not employ articles, because, as mentioned before, the Korean language does not have articles at its disposal.

[15] One might also want to consider whether the word *custody*, as used in the sign, is a potential lexical feature.

Figure 1 Subway sign in Seoul – 'Seat for the pregnant woman.'

displays the following text in English (the same information is also presented in Korean but is not reproduced here):

> Please place the valuables in our custody.
> LOTTE WORLD does not take a responsibility for the valuables lost due to guests' negligence.

Once again, we have a public sign which makes use of a plus-definite article (cf. *please place Ø valuables in our custody*). We are interested here in the two cases of "the valuables," which would identify a certain specific and/or previously identified group of valuables. Of course, the expression "your valuables" could also be used, without identifying a specific collection of valuables. But by using the plus-definite article, the referent is being specified to identifiable valuables per se, from jewelry to purses to bags, when in fact the intended referent is surely 'valuables in general/of all kinds' (placed within the stroller). Granted, we can also see the use of a zero article in reference to "guests' negligence" (and not, *the guests' negligence*), so not all possible instances on this sign do indeed use a plus-definite article. This might further suggest that plus-definite articles are potentially used when in conjunction, as outlined by Shim (1999), with a prepositional phrase (i.e., "in our custody") or when postmodified otherwise (i.e., "lost due to guests' negligence").[16]

---

[16] Note that the sign also features an instance of a plus-indefinite article ("LOTTE WORLD does not take **a** responsibility . . ."), which is not discussed here for reasons of space.

While it is easy to find more examples of plus-definite articles on signs in the South Korean landscape in our personal archives and online, we finally want to point out that the two signs which we picked for discussion here are found in public spaces which involve extremely high numbers of visitors, such as the Seoul subway or Lotte World amusement park.[17] This means that this usage is extraordinarily visible and salient. However, this should by no means be taken as a claim that all public signage in Korea displays this specific feature.

Evidence from Written Language – Academic Journal Articles

Finally, we turn to academic writing as representing a formal, generally norm-oriented, and prestigious domain. As a case in point, we draw on the *Journal of Pan-Pacific Association of Applied Linguistics* (PAAL), a Korea-based journal founded in 1999. The journal's current editor, Jaeyon Lim, is Korean, and the journal contributions are accepted in English. For our investigation of plus-definite article use, we analyzed all articles from PAAL which were authored solely by Koreans, and which were retrievable online in full – altogether sixteen. The analysis was conducted manually and consisted of a thorough examination of the complete texts of the articles, taking the context of each use into account to determine genuine uses of plus-definite articles only. Doubtful cases were excluded.

In total, 58 examples of plus-definite articles were identified across the 16 texts. The highest number of plus-definite articles in a single text was 18 and five texts did not have any instances of plus-definite articles. Examples (25) to (29) exemplify the use of plus-definite articles in this dataset.

(25) In recent years, many instructors rely on *the visual materials* as educational technology is highly desirable. (LP2008)[18]

(26) ... it was learned that the students could outperform in preparing their own presentation using *the Power Point*. (LP2008)

(27) Usually people say that they had a natural beauty, but afterwards it is revealed they had *the plastic surgery*. (L2008)

(28) To provide *the learners and ESL writers* with the appropriate teaching instruction in writing, ... (LK2013)

(29) According to *the Table 4*, the participants produced more simple words and sentences ... (P2022)

---

[17] In 2017, the Seoul metropolitan subway had an annual ridership of 1.91 billion (cf. https://en.wikipedia.org/wiki/Seoul_Metropolitan_Subway; date of access June 8, 2024). Lotte World counted 7.3 million visitors in 2016 (cf. https://en.wikipedia.org/wiki/Lotte_World; date of access June 8, 2024).

[18] As we draw on these as datapoints instead of citations, we provide examples with identifiers based on a unique letter combination and the year of publication instead of citing them.

Article SL2008, co-authored by two Korean linguists, is particularly remarkable as the use of plus-definite articles in this paper is especially frequent (n = 18). The paper reports on a study of syntactic features by Korean English language learners in a distance learning program (i.e., a second language acquisition, SLA, perspective) and, interestingly, when describing the use of articles by the participants of the study, draws on plus-definite articles as well; see (30) to (33) for a few examples.[19]

(30) However, errors in the use of ***the*** *English articles* . . . (SL2008)
(31) Thus, Koreans get confused and make lots of errors related to ***the*** *English articles* . . . (SL2008)
(32) In the syntactic features of Korean English, three different types of usages in the use of ***the*** *English articles* can be recognised . . . (SL2008)
(33) In addition, the followings are ***the*** *examples* of the misuse of 'the' when 'a/an' is needed . . . (SL2008)

Although potentially not the intention of the authors of SL2008, this aptly demonstrates how one feature can be considered an 'error' ([30] and [31]) or 'misuse' (33) when taking an SLA perspective and viewing language users as learners, while at the same time featuring in a highly formal, professional, and edited output, such as an academic journal.[20] The sheer number of plus-definite articles spread across the eleven articles indicates that this is unlikely due to matters of individual language proficiency or editorial oversight. Taken together with the evidence from spoken Korean English and the linguistic landscape, it seems like plus-definite articles could be a particularly salient part of the Korean–English morpho-syntactic repertoire, which future research could fruitfully explore further (e.g., with regard to factors potentially influencing its use, such as noun phrase complexity, mentioned but not quantified by Shim, 1999, plurality of the noun, concrete vs. abstract nouns, etc.). The existence of such patterns and features has direct implications for variety modeling and status and this is what we want to turn to in the final part of this section.

Variety Status and World Englishes Modeling

So, how do our and others' research on form inform variety status? Broadly speaking, variety status rests on a number of factors, among them historical and political aspects, language policies, speaker demographics and spread (see, e.g., Bamgbose, 1998), attitudes and functions, and, importantly, a certain

---

[19] Our excerpts stem from the main text of the article and not from the examples given by the researchers.
[20] Observant readers might have spotted other features perceived as nonstandard in the examples, for instance, the plus-plural marking in "the followings" in (33).

predictability and systematicity in terms of the respective variety's linguistic features (see, e.g., Kachru, 1983). Eventually, these forms and features are codified, for example, in dictionaries and grammar books. As Baratta (2019, 2021, 2022) has argued, beyond the traditional and 'official' means of codification just mentioned, there also exist additional possibilities for 'lay' codification, for example, online dictionaries and glossaries – and in particular these abound for the Korean context (see Baratta, 2021, for a detailed overview and examples).

It is a crucial question in World Englishes research how to identify an innovation of a form in a variety of English before its codification – when it could as well be an idiosyncratic usage or an error. Differences from L1 linguistic norms "have traditionally been characterized as 'errors' demonstrating incomplete mastery of English" (Meriläinen, 2017: 762). When looking more closely, however, the question of 'error' vs. 'innovation' is often determined by matters of variety status: L1 speakers innovate, whereas LX speakers (i.e., speakers from regions without an Anglophone postcolonial background and where English is not an official language) produce errors (and before Kachru's influential work, this was the same for postcolonial Englishes). This has recently been challenged for a number of settings, among them Cyprus (Buschfeld, 2013), the Netherlands (Edwards, 2016), and South Korea (Rüdiger, 2019). Theoretically, once a feature in a language has become widely used and accepted, it can be considered an innovation, regardless of its origins and in which variety type it is used (Li, 2010; Rosen, 2016; Baratta, 2021). We recognize that this is a long-standing debate in the field of World Englishes (and refer the interested reader to Li and He, 2021, for further discussion). In any case, however, in-depth research on linguistic forms and patterns is one of the cornerstones of World Englishes research and as this section has shown can also productively be applied to the output by Korean English users.

Considering the status of Korean English in models of World Englishes, we briefly want to mention and summarize the application of three models commonly employed by World Englishes scholars: Kachru's (1985) *Concentric Circles Model*, Schneider's (2003, 2007) *Dynamic Model of Postcolonial Englishes*, and Buschfeld and Kautzsch's (2017) *Intra- and Extraterritorial Forces (EIF) Model*.[21] Following the three-partite categorization instituted by Kachru (1985) into Inner Circle (English as a Native Language, ENL), Outer Circle (English as a Second Language, ESL), and Expanding Circle (English as a Foreign Language, EFL), South Korea is clearly classified into the Expanding

---

[21] A more detailed discussion of the variety status of Korean English can be found in Rüdiger (2019: 41–47) and Rüdiger (2020a).

Circle. Schneider's Dynamic Model of Postcolonial Englishes (henceforth Dynamic Model) is generally considered inapplicable to the Korean context, as one of the preconditions for its application (i.e., colonialism by an English-speaking force) is not fulfilled. Buschfeld and Kautzsch (2017), however, modified the Dynamic Model to cover both postcolonial and non-postcolonial Englishes and first attempts to apply the EIF Model to South Korea point toward a potential categorization of the variety between Phases 2 (Stabilization) and 3 (Nativization) (see Rüdiger, 2020a: 171). This also rests on the identification of potential linguistic features which have been nativized in the Korean context (as we have outlined in this section). While a complete overview of the extra- and intraterritorial forces is beyond the scope of this work, Rüdiger (2020a) lists the US interim military government after World War II and the extreme orientation in the society toward English (also known as 'English Fever'; see Section 1) as particularly important factors. Pop culture and tourism were also mentioned as being of special importance in the Korean context; thus, already alluding to the significance of transnational aspects, which is the main factor we want to expand on in this volume.

Conclusion

In this section, we introduced previous research on the forms of Korean English, with a main focus on (a) morpho-syntax (as this is what most research has concentrated on so far) and (b) studies conducted from a World Englishes perspective. We acknowledge the existence of a vast literature on Koreans as foreign language learners of English from the field of second language acquisition but, at the same time, emphatically want to propose a (certainly not novel) perspective taking Koreans as legitimate users of English and consider the way they use English as more than an accumulation of 'errors' in need of 'rectification.' There also exists a number of works which present forms of Korean English more anecdotally which we have not reviewed here but which may provide valuable starting points for further research (e.g., Galloway & Rose, 2015: 135–136; Takeshita, 2010). In our case study on plus-definite articles, we have traced the occurrence of this feature across modes (spoken vs. written) and genres (informal conversations, public signs, and academic writing). Last but not least, we surveyed the implications that research on forms of Korean English has for variety status and World Englishes modeling. Overall, this part of the Element has set the stage for the sections to come, which draw more extensively on original research and explore Korean–English language contact and its transnational aspects in more detail.

3 Konglish: The Life of English Loanwords in South Korea

Introduction

Another outcome of the language contact setting in South Korea (beyond the nativized forms of Korean English described in Section 2) is the proliferation of English loanwords integrated into Korean. Often, these lexical items undergo semantic and/or phonological shift and adaptation, which can be perceived as a 'mixing' of both Korean and English into what is known as Konglish. Interestingly, the term *Konglish* has also been used with many other meanings, for instance, to refer to nonstandard forms of English as used by Koreans (often pejoratively considered 'broken English') (see the references in "What About Konglish" following later in this section, in particular Kent, 1999; Hadikin, 2014: 7; and Park, 2021). In this section, we introduce different types of English loanwords and how they have been creatively appropriated by Koreans for their own purposes. English loanwords with a unique Korean flavor illustrate the agency and creativity exhibited by Koreans when it comes to integrating English lexical material into their use of Korean. In addition, we draw on questionnaire and interview data to illustrate what Koreans think about the term *Konglish* and how they report using Konglish forms themselves.

English Loanwords in Korean

The trajectories, functions, and uses of English loanwords have been examined by linguists for various Asian languages. In some contexts, such as the Japanese one, English loanwords have been described as particularly pervasive (see, e.g., Moody & Matsumoto, 2012; Scherling, 2012). In South Korea, English loanwords have also flourished, which might have been (and continues to be) facilitated by the high status of English in the Korean language ecology (cf. Park, J.-K., 2009; Song, 2012: 14; Lee, 2016). This has resulted, among other things, in an increasing Anglicization of the Korean context (Kim, S., 2024; Kim, 2021), as visible, for instance, in the linguistic landscape of Korea (Lawrence, 2012; Tan & Tan, 2015; Kim, S., 2022) but also in the Korean language itself.

In general, the Korean lexicon is of a tripartite nature: Words are either native Korean, Sino-Korean (mainly as a result of historical borrowing processes from Chinese, cf. Sohn, 2006: 44), or have been borrowed from other languages. According to Sohn (2006: 44), the ratios for modern Korean vocabulary are roughly as follows: 65 percent Sino-Korean, 30 percent native Korean, and 5 percent loanwords from other languages. Loanwords from other languages also include borrowings from non-English, mainly from languages in Asia or

Europe (e.g., 아르바이트, *areubaiteu*, from German *Arbeit*, meaning 'part-time work'; 바캉스, *bakangseu*, from French *vacance*, meaning '(a particular type of) vacation'; 돈까스, *donkkaseu*, from Japanese *tonkatsu*, a Japanese pork cutlet). However, most loanwords stem from English: "[T]he total number of current loan words [in Korean] is estimated at over 20,000, of which English occupies over 90%" (Sohn, 1999: 118). Some English loanwords were transmitted to Korean not directly from (a variety of) English but via Japanese,[22] mainly during the Japanese colonization of Korea from 1910 to 1945 (Kang, Kenstowicz & Ito, 2008: 300). This special type of loanword is sometimes referred to as *hybrid Anglo-Japanese loanword* (Tranter, 1997). In the meantime, the use of English loanwords is on the rise. Surveying corpus data consisting of articles from Korean women's magazines from 1970 to 2015, Oh and Son (2024: 428) report a "gradual and rapid increase in the usage of loanwords over time." Even though their investigation included words from other (European) languages (they mention, for example, French and German), this seems to predominantly refer to English-origin items. Similarly, Heekyung Choi (2021) found an increase in the use of English loanwords when comparing news magazine article datasets from 1991/1992 to 2011/2012.

The tripartite make-up of the Korean vocabulary also allows for the existence of lexical doublets or triplets, namely, two or three words of different origin which refer to the same semantic concept (see Table 1 for some examples).

When a Korean term already exists, the borrowing of a synonymous English loanword can influence the meaning of the Korean counterpart. In this case, the Korean lexical item can be replaced by the loanword, exist in equal distribution with the English loanword, become narrower in meaning, or its meaning can be restricted to only objects or concepts of traditional Korean design and origin (Tyson, 1993: 33). As an example for replacement of a Korean item by an English loanword, Tyson (1993: 33) mentions 카펫 (*kapet*, 'carpet'), which replaced the synonymous Korean term 양탄자 (*yangtanja*, 'carpet').

English loanwords and Korean items which exist in equal distribution are words which have "almost exactly the same meaning" and both words sound "no more or less appropriate to most Korean speakers" (Tyson, 1993: 33), as in the case of 장화 (*janghwa*, 'boots') and the English loanword 부츠 (*bucheu*, 'boots'). Instead of existing synonymously, the Korean term can also become restricted in meaning. This can be illustrated with 전산기 (*jeonsangi*, 'computing machine, calculating machine'), which used to refer to every kind of computing machine but became narrower in meaning when the English

---

[22] Additionally, many Chinese lexical items were also borrowed to Korean via Japanese (see Tranter, 1997).

Table 1 Native/English loan and Sino-Korean/English loan doublets and native/ Sino-Korean/English loan triplets (examples taken from Sohn, 1999: 117).

Native	Sino-Korean	English loan	Meaning
-	정구 *jeonggu*	테니스 *teniseu*	'tennis'
-	사진기 *sajingi*	카메라 *kamera*	'camera'
단추 *danchu*	-	버튼 *beoteun*	'button'
튀긴 *twigin*	-	프라이 *peurai*	'frying, fried food'
춤 *chum*	무용 *muyong*	댄스 *daenseu*	'dance'
비옷 *biot*	우의 *uui*	레인코트 *reinkoteu*	'raincoat'

loanword 컴퓨터 (*keompyuteo*, 'computer') was introduced. Nowadays, 전산기 (*jeonsangi*) usually refers to a calculator specifically. Frequently, the Korean term refers to concepts or objects which are considered traditionally Korean whereas the English loanword is used to refer to the westernized counterpart. The Korean term 여관 (*yeogwan*), for example, refers to Korean-style hotels whereas the English loanword 호텔 (*hotel*) designates (originally) Western-style lodging.

There are also cases where lexical doublets exist because a Korean word is introduced to accompany or replace an English loanword that was originally borrowed to fill a lexical gap. This is usually related to efforts to 'purify' the Korean language. Eun-Yong Kim (2022), for instance, reports on the efforts of the Language Purification Committee (말다듬기 위원회, *maldadeumgi wiwonhoe*), which proposes and promotes 'replacement words' for popular foreign terms in South Korea. For example, 플리마켓 (*peullimaket*, 'flea market') is to be replaced with 벼룩 시장 (*byeoruk sijang*) and 골든타임 (*goldeuntaim*, 'golden time')[23] with 황금 시간 (*hwanggeum sigan*) (examples from Kim, E.-Y., 2022). However, drawing on large-scale diachronic corpora of Korean, Eun-Yong Kim (2022: 141) found that these artificially introduced replacement words are not successful in replacing the English loanwords, which shows that matters of language codification ultimately go beyond institutional efforts and are in need of acceptance by the people who use the language (Baratta, 2021).

---

[23] 골든타임 (*goldeuntaim*, 'golden time') refers to the perfect time to do something.

Generally, loanwords from English (and any other language) must conform to Korean syllable construction and pronunciation rules. This often results in vowel epenthesis at the end of syllables (Cho & Park, 2006: 241), as, for example, found in 스트라이크 (*seuteuraikeu*, 'strike'), where the consonant cluster [st] that cannot be realized in Korean is resolved by inserting the epenthetic vowel [ɨ] (ㅡ) after [s] (ㅅ) and before [t] (ㅌ) (and the same happens again to resolve [tr]). Other adaptive processes include the splitting of English diphthongs [aɪ], [aʊ], and [ɔɪ] into two syllables (Nam & Southard, 1994: 267) (also observable in *seuteuraikeu*, 'strike') and the replacement of consonant sounds which are absent in Korean phonology, such as the dental fricatives [ð] and [θ], the labiodental fricatives [v] and [f], and the alveolar fricative [z], by the "corresponding stop or [plain or glottalized] fricative sounds" (Sohn, 1999: 117). Some examples for the replacement of fricatives in loanwords from English in Korean can be found in 소파 (*sopa*, 'sofa'), 퀴즈 (*kwijeu*, 'quiz'), and 바이올린 (*baiollin*, 'violin'). These changes in pronunciation present a contrast to the original English and make the words easily recognizable as 'Koreanized.'

Additionally, English loanwords in Korean can be categorized based on the amount of semantic and morphological change involved in their adaptation (see, e.g., Kent, 1999; Kim, 2012).[24] This can range from no change (beyond the adaptation of spelling and pronunciation outlined previously), also known as *direct loans*, to changes such as semantic shift, creative compounding, mixed-code combinations, and clipping (see Kim, 2012). An overview of the different loanword types plus examples can be found in the following list. While the list only presents rather clear-cut cases, there are also possibilities for some categories to combine or overlap. For example, the Korean word 아파트 (*apateu*, lit. 'apart') illustrates a combination of clipping (*apartment > apart*) and semantic shift (English: 'apartment/flat'; Korean: 'a complete apartment building').

(a) direct
  오렌지 (*orenji*; from English *orange* [fruit])
  이메일 (*imeil*; from English *email*)
  와인 (*wain*; from English *wine*)
(b) semantic shift
  탤런트 (*taelleonteu*; from English *talent* = 'celebrity')

---

[24] In addition, we can distinguish between lexical items that were borrowed to fill a lexical gap and substitution, where the new word from English "replace[s] existing Korean terminology" (Kent, 1999: 202). These terms include for example: 라이터 (*raiteo*, 'lighter') replacing the Korean term 불 (*bul*, 'lighter') and 파킹 (*paking*, 'parking') replacing the Korean term 주차 (*jucha*, 'parking').

빌라 (*billa*; from English *villa* = 'apartment unit')

스탠드 (*seutaendeu*; from English *stand* = 'lamp')

(c) creative compounding

아이 쇼핑 (*ai syoping*; from English *eye shopping* = 'window shopping')

백미러 (*baekmireo*; from English *back mirror* = 'rearview mirror')

(d) mixed-code combinations

안전 벨트 (*anjeon belteu*; Korean word for 'safety' + English *belt* = 'safety belt')

감자 칩 (*gamja chip*; Korean word for 'potato' + English *chip* = 'potato chip')

(e) clipping

셀카 (*selka*; clipping of English *self-camera* to *sel-ka* = 'selfie')

매스 컴 (*maeseu keom*; clipping of English *mass communication* to *mass com* = 'media')

(from Rüdiger, 2018: 188; based on Kim, 2012)

Regarding semantic change, Tyson (1993: 32) observed three possible processes for English loanwords in Korea: Semantic narrowing (also known as restriction), semantic widening (also known as extension), and semantic transfer (also known as semantic shift). Semantic narrowing can, for example, be found in the lexical item 미팅 (*miting*, 'meeting') (this and all following examples from Tyson, 1993: 32). Whereas the OED defines *meeting* as the general "act or an instance of assembling or coming together for social, business, or other purposes; the action of encountering a person or persons" (OED, n.d. 'meeting'), the English loanword in Korean denotes a 'blind date' (so a specific type of coming together only) and has therefore been restricted in meaning. Semantic widening refers to the opposite process. The English term *service*, when used as the loanword 서비스 (*seobiseu*, lit. 'service'), acquires the extended meaning of "anything offered free of charge" (Tyson, 1993: 32). Semantic transfer often results in a meaning which is still related to the original lexical field. While 매니큐어 (*maenikyueo*, lit. 'manicure'), for example, refers to fingernail polish and not to the "cosmetic treatment and care of the hands and fingernails; an instance of such treatment, esp. by a manicurist; the state of the hands and fingernails resulting from this treatment" (OED, n.d. 'manicure'), we can easily file both meanings into the same semantic field.

The loanwords which draw on semantic creativity (i.e., those involving semantic shift and/or creative compounding) are not only the ones usually picked up on in the press and lay discourses[25] but can also be considered

---

[25] See, for example, the Reddit thread "List of essential Konglish" (posted on the subreddit r/Korea); available at www.reddit.com/r/Korean/comments/m1foee/list_of_essential_konglish/.

most interesting for World Englishes researchers as they illustrate processes of linguistic adaptation and agency. A few additional, well-known, examples are:

- 커닝 (*keoning*, lit. 'cunning,' 'cheating (in a test)')
- 핸드폰 (*haendeupon*, lit. 'handphone,' 'mobile phone')
- 원샷 (*wonsyat*, lit. 'one shot,' 'bottom's up!')
- 노트 (*noteu*, lit. 'note,' 'notebook')
- 화이트 (*hwaiteu*, lit. 'white,' 'correction fluid')

In some cases, these items have been derogatively designated as 'pseudo-loanwords' (Kent, 1999) or even 'misused' English words (Ahn, 2000; cited in Duffy, 2003: 36). However, they play an important role for the expression of cultural identity and speakers' linguistic agency, and, according to Lee (1986: 198), they "deliver the Korean feeling and carry the weight of Korean experience with an altered form and meaning to suit to new Korean surroundings." Another word that is at times used for these specific lexical items is *Konglish* (see Rüdiger, 2018: 188), and it is this term that we will turn to next.

What About Konglish?

The term *Konglish* (a blend of the words *Korean* and *English*), as also introduced at the beginning of this Element, has been used with various meanings, one of them (i.e., Korean English loanwords involving semantic change and linguistic creativity) has just been introduced. But what exactly is understood as Konglish differs. Originally, the term seems to implicate a form of code-mixing and forms part of a general pattern to designate 'language blending': *Japlish* stands for *Japanese + English*, *Chinglish* for *Chinese + English*, and *Denglish* for *Deutsch* ('German') + *English*. Taking a closer look at the term *Chinglish*, we can observe it being used with a clearly negative connotation (see Qiang & Wolff, 2003). Eaves (2011) explicitly differentiates between three clearly related but nevertheless distinct terms: *Chinese English* (a learner variety of English), *China English* (a new, emerging variety of World Englishes), and *Chinglish* (the English mistakes in translation or expression found in the Chinese linguistic landscape). Accordingly, Schneider (2014: 19) reports a division introduced by Chinese scholars between *China English*, which is largely evaluated positively and accepted, and *Chinglish* (or *Chinese English*) which "refer[s] to an interlanguage, often with pejorative connotations." This is also reflected by Henry (2010) who believes that Chinglish, "a perceived incorrect or deformed version of Standard English" (669), is a "particular

---

Searching for *Konglish* on Reddit reveals numerous threads of interest for further exploration of language attitudes and notions of 'correctness.'

metadiscursive construction rather than a clearly defined linguistic variant" (686).

For the South Korean context, a similar plethora of terms exists, among them *Konglish, Korean English, Koreanized English,* and *English in Korea.* In particular *Konglish* is used throughout the literature with various meanings, which we want to unravel in the following.

(1) *Konglish as Koreanized English Variety*
Some scholars use *Konglish* to refer to a Koreanized variety of English. Jamie Shinhee Lee (2014: 35), for example, describes Konglish as "'Korean-style' English" and Sangsup Lee (1989: 36) asserts that Konglish stands for Korean English which shows substrate language influence from Korean.

(2) *Konglish as Learner English*
Other scholars use *Konglish* to refer to a learner variety of English as used by Korean speakers (see, e.g., Honna, 2006: 124, who states that Konglish is "a coinage that refers to patterns of English Korean students tend to employ"). Emphasis here lies on the 'learner aspect' and the subsequent classification of nonstandard forms as errors.

(3) *Konglish as Mixture of Substrate Language Influence and Interlanguage Effects*
Park (2010: 200–201) concedes that there is no exact definition of Konglish and states that it "is generally assumed to refer to the 'broken' English that arises from interference from Korean and a superficial training in English." In other words, Konglish is seen as the result of the substrate language influence of Korean and learners' mistakes. Lawrence (2012) takes a similar position in seeing a relation of Konglish to interlanguage effects as well as substrate language influence. He supports the notion that it is difficult to define but adds that it is "a spoken, not codified, language" which is "often defined via vocabulary, sometimes via grammar, sometimes via pronunciation, and sometimes simply classed as 'bad English'" (Lawrence, 2012: 72).

(4) *Konglish as Lexical Set*
Kent (1999: 198) uses *Konglish* to refer to the "loan terminology stemming from English, [*sic*] and European languages" used in South Korea. This is also the usage which we have adopted, with the additional reference to semantic and/or phonetic change.

(5) *Konglish as a Cultural Practice*
More recently, Park (2021: 138) has conceptualized Konglish as a cultural practice, "in which Koreans draw upon whatever resource available to them

in making communicative action, and through which Koreans conceptualize their position in the global world."

In our own writing (including the present manuscript), we use the term
Konglish in the sense of (4) ('Konglish as a Lexical Set'; with particular reference
to words which have undergone semantic and/or phonetic change). In contrast,
Korean English refers to the variety of English used by South Koreans, that is,
subsuming variation on all linguistic levels. This includes lexical variation and
could, theoretically, also involve the use of Konglish words. However, as there is
no evidence for this so far[26] we continue to use *Konglish* as defined in (4).

The differing conceptualization and perception of Konglish[27] by scholars
leaves the question open as to what Korean people themselves understand under
the term *Konglish*, and how they report using it. To this end, the first author
conducted two small-scale studies based on in-depth interviews (with 14 participants, mainly on definitions of Konglish) and online questionnaires (with 74
participants, mainly on attitudes and on usage).[28] The attitude results are
reported on in Rüdiger (2018), but here we want to draw on the unpublished
self-reported usage and interview data. More information, particularly on the
questionnaire data, can be found in Rüdiger (2018).

When asked to define *Konglish*, not surprisingly, all interview participants
referred to the fact that Konglish is based on both English and Korean, saying,
for example, that it is "Korean and English together" (given by a female English
education student) or a "combined language like with English and Korean"
(as uttered by a female student of French literature and psychology). For most of
the participants (i.e., 9 out of 14), Konglish operated exclusively on the lexical
level, echoing our application of the term. More specifically, they explained that
Konglish refers to English words that are used when speaking Korean and
which have undergone semantic change. Three participants additionally mentioned pronunciation as a relevant factor in Konglish (i.e., the fact that Korean
syllable structure and other pronunciation rules need to be followed when
borrowing words from English; see the beginning of this section). Two participants mentioned that Konglish also works on other linguistic levels besides

---

[26] For example, in all of SPOKE, no established Konglish words were found. It should be
mentioned though that SPOKE might be too small for this type of analysis, and semantic shift
and lexis in Korean English remain to be investigated in detail.

[27] In its 2021 K-update (see Section 4), the *Oxford English Dictionary* team also added *Konglish*,
which is defined there as "[a] mixture of Korean and English, esp. an informal hybrid language
spoken by Koreans, incorporating elements of Korean and English" (OED, n.d. 'Konglish').

[28] The interview participants were students, largely female (13 women vs. 1 man), and aged 19–29.
The online questionnaire participants were students and early professionals, 41 women and 33
men, aged 18–48. Both groups subsumed students studying English education but also a range of
other subjects and professions. All data was collected in the early 2010s.

Table 2 Self-reported use of Konglish by questionnaire participants.

Would you use Konglish words when speaking to ...	Yes	No	Don't know	N/A	Additional comment
... your grandparents?	34	24	12	4	35
... your parents?	58	9	3	4	28
... a teacher or professor?	37	23	10	4	29

lexis (such as pragmatics). While arguably a small sample, it seems as if Korean speakers themselves do conceptualize Konglish primarily as relating to lexical resources, specifically English loanwords which have undergone mainly semantic (but also phonological) changes to adapt to the Korean linguistic and cultural system. Meaning (4) and (5) from the list ('Konglish as a Lexical Set' and 'Konglish as Cultural Practice') thus seem to be most relevant to the speakers themselves.

The questionnaire which was subsequently administered (to a different subject group) therefore specifically focused on Konglish as a lexical resource. Among other questions, participants were prompted to state whether they would use Konglish words when speaking to their grandparents, their parents, and teachers or professors. The questionnaire allowed only three options as answers ("yes," "no," and "don't know"), but participants also had the possibility to leave an optional comment (which was used by around half of the respondents). An overview of the responses can be found in Table 2.

While self-reported data potentially tells us more about what participants think they do, rather than what they actually do, this allowed for the elicitation of interesting meta-linguistic statements, revealing participants' ideas and conceptualizations of Konglish.

Using Konglish Words with Grandparents

Nearly 50 percent of the participants specified that they would use Konglish words when talking to their grandparents. In the comments, participants, for example, stated that grandparents would not know the difference between English and Konglish words in any case, and it therefore does not matter whether one uses a Konglish or a 'proper' English word when talking to them (see [1]). Note how this rests on the assumption that the participants' grandparents are familiar with Konglish words and their meanings, as the potential problem is not that grandparents do not understand but that they might be irritated by the semantic change.

(1)   My grandparents don't know anything about English, so I think it can be okay to use Konglish words to others (P45m)[29]

This sentiment can also be found expressed in example (2) where the respondent claims that contrary to English per se, Konglish words are known by the older generations.

(2)   they also can understand Konglish and many words used nowadays are Konglish mostly (P30f)

The participants who stated that they would *not* use Konglish words with their grandparents, however, mostly argued that their grandparents cannot understand Konglish, which contradicts (1) and (2). Nevertheless, none of the participants implied that it would be disrespectful or impolite to use Konglish words with their grandparents as such.

Using Konglish Words with Parents

Most participants would use Konglish words with their parents (nearly 83 percent). Participant 12, a male engineering student, additionally emphasized the more positive aspects associated with Konglish, as "Konglish is more humorous and funny." Some parents use Konglish words themselves (see [3]), so their children see no reason to avoid these words when talking to them.

(3)   Because they also use kind of Konglish (P34f)

In general, parents are considered to be "well adapted" (P11f) to and familiar with the use of Konglish. None of the participants stated fearing problems in understanding or politeness issues when using Konglish words with their parents. Only one participant stated that he does not like resorting to Konglish when talking to his parents because he felt too conservative for it (P39m).

Using Konglish Words with Teachers or Professors

More than half of the participants would use Konglish words with their educators, but those who stated that they would not use Konglish words with teachers and professors are very stern in rejecting this notion. Whereas the main reason for not using Konglish with grandparents was the idea that the grandparents might not understand the considerably younger speakers, now the main issue is one of formality and appearing professional (see [4]).

---

[29]   Participant identifiers include participant number; f = female respondent, m = male respondent. The examples retain original spelling.

(4) **Absolutely not**. If it is a serious, academic environment, It [I] would **never** use Konglish because it might make me **feel ashamed of myself** for being aware whether it was Konglish or not. . . . (P5f, emphasis added)

Excerpt (4) demonstrates clearly that there is no case in which this participant would use Konglish with a teacher or professor (expressed via the extreme case formulations "absolutely not" and "never"). The use of Konglish words in a formal setting (such as academia) evokes very strong negative emotions in her, as she would "feel ashamed." A potential explanation for her strong opinion toward this subject could lie in her majoring in English education (which presumably is geared toward a more conservative perspective on language use and change). Even though this participant also expressed a negative opinion when asked about her attitude toward Konglish directly, she nevertheless reported using Konglish with her parents and even grandparents, which indicates a differentiation between private and more professional settings.

Likewise, other participants asserted that Konglish words might make them appear unprofessional (P73f, a flight attendant, a profession which relies on effective communication across cultural and linguistic backgrounds), and many tried to be "careful" (P62f) and find an "original expression" (P50f, English education) instead. Participant 12 also rejected the use of Konglish in a formal setting and asserted that "[u]sing appropriate word is the one of the factor of the educated people" (P12m).[30]

Nevertheless, the group of participants who report using Konglish words with their educators is in the majority. Some of the reasons given are the efficiency and the prevalence of Konglish words in Korean society and language. P34f, a student of English education, contradicting (4), stated that "it is common to use Konglish in Korea even if we are in quite formal setting." It also seems to depend on the addressee: P48f (economics) specified not to use Konglish when talking to foreign professors, P29m (English education) would not use it when talking to a professor of the Korean language, and P66f (English literature) asserted that she would use Konglish words only if she heard the professor using Konglish as well.

The word *Konglish* is frequently used together with adjectives with negative semantic connotation resulting in a negative connotation associated with the term itself: Konglish has been termed "bad English" (Lawrence, 2012: 72), "broken English" (Park, 2010: 200–201), and "incorrect English" (Park, J. S.-Y., 2009: 109). Ahn (2014: 205) showed that Korean teachers of English identify Konglish as "inappropriate" and "not real," whereas Korean English (i.e., a Korean-style variety of English as described for instance in Section 2; cf. also Ahn, 2014: 203) was closely linked to Korean identity and was labeled

---

[30] Readers might note the use of plus-definite articles in this answer (see Section 2).

"unique" and "sophisticated." Hadikin (2014: 7) reports that simply mentioning the term *Konglish* with students can result in "a chorus of giggles" which leads him to conclude that he has "the sense that few students would openly admit to being a Konglish user." Surprisingly then, participants of this survey quite openly admitted to using Konglish, not only when speaking to their parents (admittedly, a quite familiar domain of language use) but also when talking to their grandparents (which due to the gap in age and hierarchy traditionally calls for the use of more polite speech styles in Korean), and even when interacting with teachers and/or professors in formal settings. The main reasons for not using Konglish with teachers/professors were the formal (academic) setting whereas with grandparents, some (but by no means all) participants stated that they expected problems in understanding, which prevented them from using Konglish. It seems that the main influencing factor here is the formality of the situation. The reported usage rates indicate that Konglish words are becoming more and more integrated in the Korean language and are starting to, at least partially, lose their negative connotations. The negative issues though are still visible when it comes to contexts where one needs to appear professional, such as talking to professors or teachers, but not when talking to parents or grandparents where one would still like to appear polite but does not need to prove one's professional manners. Further studies might want to corroborate the findings from this study by inquiring into the use of Konglish with other social groups, such as friends, strangers of different age groups, and co-workers.[31] Taken in their entirety, these findings complicate the notion of Konglish, as previously reported in the literature. However, any judgments of such lexis, whether positive or negative, while important considerations, are separate from what is otherwise a value- and judgment-free definition: Konglish is a lexical set of specific English-based words used by Koreans, mainly when speaking Korean. The question of how far Konglish lexis is employed in Korean English is unclear, as the datasets that are currently available are either too small for dedicated work on the lexical level (see footnote 26) or too restricted in the contexts they represent.

Conclusion

English loanwords not only testify to processes of Anglicization in the Korean setting, but they also demonstrate Korean speakers' agency and creativity, in particular when semantic shift is concerned. While these loanwords are met

---

[31] Note again that this study only analyzed the self-reported willingness of participants to employ Konglish words with certain interlocutor groups. Even if participants stated that, for example, they do not use Konglish with their grandparents, this does not mean that participants do not do so when actually talking to their grandparents. This could be investigated via extensive recording of actual conversations between the respective groups in natural settings.

with 'mixed feelings' (see Rüdiger, 2018), they are also valued for their Koreanness and for forming part of a cultural practice (see Park, 2021, on Konglish as a cultural practice). As for the often pejoratively used term *Konglish*, it turns out that for the Koreans surveyed in this section, this refers to a lexical set of Koreanized English words, which are not necessarily seen negatively. They are mainly reported as being used independently of status of interlocutor, rather depending on the formality of the situation and the individual's preferences. In true transnational fashion, Konglish words can also be re-borrowed into and used in English, and in fact, this has happened with several terms (even on an institutionalized level involving the *Oxford English Dictionary*) – we will come to this in the next section along with other Korean lexical phenomena in English.

4 The *K*-World: Korean Lexis in English

Introduction

In this section, we turn to the other side of the coin of Korean–English language contact, namely, the influence which Korean has had on the use of English worldwide. This contrasts with the previous section which looked at English loanwords used in Korean, as we now consider the use of Korean words by English speakers around the globe. Facilitated by the extreme success of Korean pop culture products (known as *hallyu* the 'Korean Wave', cf., e.g., Marinescu, 2014; Lee & Nornes, 2015; Jin, Yoon & Min, 2021; see also Section 5), the Korean language has left significant lexical traces on English. This is for example attested by the inclusion of numerous Korean loanwords in the *Oxford English Dictionary* (OED), which in 2021 added twenty-six new words of Korean origin (Salazar, n.d.). Notably, these words go beyond food items and physical cultural artefacts and also include, for example, terms of address (e.g., *oppa*, *noona*) and discourse markers and interjections (e.g., *daebak*, *fighting*). In this section, we use two corpora, namely, the *Global Web-based English Corpus* (GloWbE) and the *News on the Web Corpus* (NOW), to investigate the spread of Korean vocabulary in Inner and Outer Circle Englishes. In addition, we present a study on the use of the *K*-prefix, which is most famously found in *K-pop* but which has become very productive. Drawing on NOW, we show that this item not only evokes the success of K-pop but has become an iconic means for creating references to the Korean context.

Korean Words and the *Oxford English Dictionary*

Using the advanced search function of the OED returns forty-one entries with 'Korean' as language of origin. The announcement on the OED blog

(Salazar, n.d.) lists an additional six items which are not returned with the search function, four of which are realistically to be classified as words related to Korea and Korean phenomena, but not necessarily as Korean loanwords (i.e., the prefix *K-*, *K-drama*, *Konglish*, and *Korean wave*, which we do not include here; the *K*-prefix is treated in detail in the last part of this section). Table 3 lists all of the forty-three Korean loanwords which can be found in the OED, thematically subcategorized into 'food and drink' (fourteen items; note that Kiaer, 2021, only listed five items in this category), 'address terms' (three items), 'sports' (three items), 'literature, music, and pop culture' (six items), and 'other' (seventeen items). While we focus in this section on their status as loanwords into English (as given in the OED), they can be found used in other languages too (for instance, *Kimchi* is also an entry in the German *Duden*; cf. Duden, n.d. 'Kimchi'). Note that the OED does not limit the usage of the loanwords to a specific variety of English. This means they are considered part of a general English 'word stock' and not restricted to a specific variety – such as American English or Australian English, or indeed Korean English, a variety of English where these items are, of course, also used.

The first years of attestation in the OED show that the adoption of Korean loanwords into English is by no means a recent phenomenon – with the oldest

Table 3 Korean loanwords listed in the *Oxford English Dictionary* (ordered alphabetically with first year of attestation in brackets).

Category	Korean Loanwords in the OED
Food and drink	*banchan* (1938), *bibimbap* (1977), *bulgogi* (1958), *chimaek* (2012), *doenjang* (1966), *dongchimi* (1962), *galbi* (1958), *gochujang* (1966), *japchae* (1955), *kimbap* (1966), *kimchi* (1888), *soju* (1951), *makkoli* (1970), *samgyeopsal* (1993)
Address terms	*noona* (1975), *oppa* (1963), *unni* (1997)
Sports	*hapkido* (1963), *taekwondo* (1962), *Tang Soo Do* (1957)
Literature, music, and pop culture	*gisaeng* (1894), *hallyu* (2003), *manhwa* (1988), *mukbang* (2013), *sijo* (1986), *trot* (1986)
Other	*aegyo* (1997), *chaebol* (1972), *daebak* (2003), *fighting* (2002), *hagwon* (1988), *hanbok* (1952), *Hangul* (1935), *Juche* (1963), *Kono* (1895), *myon* (1898), *ondol* (1935), *onmun* (1882), *PC bang* (1999), *ri* (1817), *skinship* (1966), *won* (1947), *yangban* (1888)

item (*ri*, a unit of length) attested as early as 1817. Taking a closer look at the four example attestations for *kimchi* in the OED, we see that while earlier examples typographically marked *kimchi* as a foreign word by enclosing it in single quotation marks (see [a]) or setting it in italics (see [b]) and explaining its meaning in the text ("a peculiar kind of pickle resembling sauer kraut" in [a] and "an unbelievably 'hot' pickle" in [b]), this is not the case for the latter attestations given in (c) and (d).

(a) There is a peculiar kind of pickle resembling sauer kraut which goes by the name of **'kimchi'**.

   1888, *Gospel in All Lands August 366/2*

(b) A unique part of the diet and important for its vitamin content is *kimchi*, an unbelievably 'hot' pickle.

   1966, *S. McCune, Korea iv. 33*

(c) Signature dishes: pork and **kimchi** pancake.

   2014, *48 Hours 27 February 59/3*

(d) Recently receiving some homemade **kimchi** from a friend, I knew what I wanted to do with it . . . It may not sound right, but a gooey grilled cheese is the perfect pairing for spicy, garlicky **kimchi**.

   2019, *Fairbanks (Alaska) Daily News-Miner 25 September b3/1*

   (all examples from OED, n.d. 'kimchi'; bold emphasis added)

We also want to briefly point to five vocabulary items from Table 3 that are particularly relevant in illustrating Korean–English language contact and the mutual influences between the two languages: *chimaek, PC bang, fighting, trot,* and *skinship*. All five items include English-language elements (with *fighting, trot,* and *skinship* classifiable as Konglish words, as they are originally English loanwords into Korean which have undergone semantic change):

- *chimaek* is a blend of English *chicken* and Korean 맥주, *maekju* ('beer') and refers to a popular meal consisting of fried chicken served with beer (note that the English loanword 치킨, *chikin* 'chicken' in Korea means 'fried chicken')
- *PC bang* is a compound of English *PC* and Korean 방, *bang* ('room') and designates a kind of internet café (often used for playing video games)
- *fighting* is originally an English word which was borrowed into Korean (화이팅; *hwaiting*),[32] which was subsequently reborrowed (with changed grammatical status and meaning) back into English as an interjection "expressing encouragement, incitement, or support" (OED, n.d. 'fighting')

---

[32] As Korean does have neither letter <f> nor sound /f/, the loanword was modified to start with <h>, /h/.

- *trot* is a clipping of the English word *foxtrot* and refers to a specifically Korean genre of music (influenced by American, European, and Japanese popular music styles; cf. OED, n.d. 'trot')
- *skinship* is a blend of the words *skin* and *kinship*; the OED defines it as "touching or close physical contact between parent and child or (esp. in later use) between lovers or friends, used to express affection or strengthen an emotional bond" (OED, n.d. 'skinship').[33]

In the following, we want to go beyond dictionary evidence and investigate the spread of Korean words in two English-language corpora: The *Global Web-based English Corpus* and the *News on the Web Corpus*.

Korean Words in Inner and Outer Circle Englishes

The *Global Web-based English Corpus* (GloWbE) consists of 1.9 billion words of (largely informal) online material, such as websites and blogs published in twenty English-language speaking countries (GloWbE, n.d.). This includes the six Inner Circle contexts (i.e., United States, Canada, Great Britain, Ireland, Australia, and New Zealand) and fourteen Outer Circle contexts (i.e., India, Sri Lanka, Pakistan, Bangladesh, Singapore, Malaysia, the Philippines, Hong Kong, South Africa, Nigeria, Ghana, Kenya, Tanzania, and Jamaica). More information on the corpus can be found in Davies and Fuchs (2015). It should be mentioned here that the corpus data were collected at the end of 2012 and thus can only give us a glimpse at how Korean words were employed by internet users in the 2000s and very early 2010s. While some Korean pop culture products were already popular by then, this remained a somewhat niche interest, with the Korean Wave gaining much more ground in the late 2010s (consider, for example, that the immensely popular song *Gangnam Style* by artist Psy was released in October 2012; the Korean boyband sensation BTS debuted in 2013; see also Section 5 on the spread of Korean pop culture around the world). We therefore supplement the GloWbE data with the *News on the Web Corpus* (NOW; cf. NOW, n.d.), which has the disadvantage of covering a different genre (online news reports) but as a monitor corpus provides up-to-date information (in our case from 2010 to mid-April 2024, which was the time when we conducted our corpus searches). In addition, while a form of institutionalized discourse, it is interesting to survey the use of Korean words in English-language media as these texts can be considered multipliers for the use of specific lexical items. NOW also provides the same regional distinctions as the GloWbE corpus, and thus makes it ideal as a further

---

[33] The OED predates this usage and attributes it to Japanese origin; however, this item was explicitly listed in Salazar's blog post on the OED as having been included as part of the 'K-update.'

point of reference for our study. At the time of conducting the corpus queries, NOW was 18.9 billion words in size. As we will illustrate, differences in the results from GloWbE and NOW can potentially be related to the timeframe and genres covered by each corpus – with, for instance, news media picking up on different aspects and topics than blogs and websites.

We consider here most of the items which were added in the 2021 K-update to the OED: *aegyo, banchan, bulgogi, chimaek, daebak, dongchimi, galbi, hallyu, hanbok, japchae, kimbap, manhwa, mukbang, noona, oppa, PC bang, samgyeopsal, skinship,* and *Tang Soo Do.* We excluded *fighting* and *trot* due to the necessity to manually disambiguate them from their other meanings, which, combined with their high frequency (*fighting* in GloWbE n = 116,371, in NOW n = 1,283,074; *trot* in GloWbE n = 3,157, in NOW n = 26,520), was not feasible for our purposes. *Unni* had to be excluded as it overlapped largely with its use as a (non-Korean) first name. The *K*-prefix is investigated in detail in the next part of this section. We did not take spelling variation into account (e.g., *kimbap* vs. *kimbab, mukbang* vs. *meokbang, galbi* vs. *kalbi*) but searched for the spelling given in the OED only. Additional lemmas and compounded forms were searched for using wildcards (e.g., *aegyo**). All wildcard search results were manually disambiguated to exclude false hits. Proper names that included the search term and had a relationship to Korea were retained (e.g., *Hallyumart,* which is a business selling K-pop outfits).

For reasons of space, we report the results in two separate tables: Table 4 for GloWbE and Table 5 for NOW. Frequencies are given for the exact word form, with additional lemmas and compounded forms given in a separate column (i.e., lemma and compound form frequencies are not included in the total raw frequency). The top 3 regional users column gives the raw frequency of the lexical item in the respective context, the frequency per million words, and the percentage of all uses in the corpus. The order is determined by the frequency per million words (pmw). In case of equal pmw, the variety with higher raw frequency is listed first (cases of equal pmw and raw frequency are listed jointly).

Nearly all of the 2021 Korean loanword additions to the OED that were searched for in GloWbE were found, with the exception of *chimaek* and *mukbang.* The main users according to GloWbE are located in Asia, with Singapore and the Philippines usually found in the top 3. Hong Kong and Malaysia also play important roles, but there are also other contexts which feature in the top 3s, such as the USA (for *aegyo* and *Tang Soo Do*) and South Africa (for *galbi*). Other top 3 regional users are located, for instance, in Great Britain, New Zealand, Canada, Australia, India, and Nigeria, but this is mainly the case for low frequency items (e.g., *dongchimi,* a kind of radish kimchi, with

Table 4 Korean loanwords used in GloWbE.

Lexical item	Freq. in GloWbE raw total (+ pmw)	Top 3 users in GloWbE (raw frequency/ frequency per million words/percent of all uses in the corpus)	Additional lemmas and combined forms in GloWbE
aegyo	133 (0.07)	1. Singapore (92/2.14/69 percent) 2. Malaysia (26/0.62/20 percent) 3. United States (13/0.03/10 percent)	*aegyos* (verb, 3rd person present tense), *aegyo-laced, aegyo-fied, aegyo-punching, aegyoness, aegyo-y, aegyo-Yoona, aegyo-tastic, aegyo-speak, aegyo-noona, aegyo-answers, aegyo-ish, aegyo-free, aegyo-light, aegyo-filled*
banchan	52 (0.03)	1. Hong Kong (8/0.20/15 percent) 2. the Philippines (7/0.16/13 percent) 3. Singapore (5/0.12/10 percent)	*banchans* (noun, plural)
bulgogi	224 (0.12)	1. the Philippines (116/2.68/52 percent) 2. Malaysia (34/0.82/15 percent) 3. Singapore (10/0.23/4 percent)	-
chimaek	-	-	-
daebak	99 (0.05)	1. Singapore (65/1.51/66 percent) 2. Malaysia (24/0.58/24 percent) 3. the Philippines (6/0.14/6 percent)	*daebakkk, daebakk, Daebaksubs*

Term	Count (percentage)	Countries	Derived forms
dongchimi	3 (0.00)	1. Hong Kong (1/0.02/33 percent) 2. Canada (2/0.01/67 percent)	–
galbi	38 (0.02)	1. South Africa (12/0.26/32 percent) 2. the Philippines (6/0.18/16 percent) 3. Hong Kong (8/0.15/21 percent)	*Galbisal*
hallyu	440 (0.23)	1. Malaysia (182/4.37/41 percent) 2. Singapore (158/3.68/36 percent) 3. the Philippines (36/0.83/8 percent)	*hallyuwood, hallyu-concerts, hallyu-related, hallyuback, hallyu-of-the-North, hallyu-idol*
hanbok	85 (0.04)	1. Singapore (37/0.86/44 percent) 2. Malaysia (19/0.46/22 percent) 3. the Philippines (6/0.14/7 percent)	*hanboks* (noun, plural), *hanbok-clad*
japchae	13 (0.01)	1. the Philippines (6/0.14/46 percent) 2. Hong Kong (1/0.02/8 percent) 3. Malaysia (1/0.02/8 percent)	–
kimbap	43 (0.02)	1. Malaysia (17/0.41/40 percent) 2. Singapore (8/0.19/19 percent) 3. the Philippines (2/0.05/5 percent)	–
manhwa	41 (0.02)	1. Singapore (16/0.37/39 percent) 2. Malaysia (4/0.10/10 percent) 3. the Philippines (2/0.05/5 percent)	*manhwas* (noun, plural), *manhwa-ka*
mukbang	–	–	–
noona	253 (0.13)	1. Singapore (173/4.03/68 percent) 2. Malaysia (59/1.42/23 percent)	*noonas* (noun, plural), *noona-dongs(a)eng, noona-killer, noona-is-my-lover, noona-girlfriend, noona-slayer,*

Table 4 (cont.)

Lexical item	Freq. in GloWbE raw total (+ pmw)	Top 3 users in GloWbE (raw frequency/ frequency per million words/percent of all uses in the corpus)	Additional lemmas and combined forms in GloWbE
		3. the Philippines (14/0.32/6 percent)	*noona-romance, roona-pout-wiggle, noona-loving, noona-love, noona-celebrity*
oppa	772 (0.41)	1. Singapore (393/9.14/51 percent) 2. Malaysia (204/4.90/26 percent) 3. the Philippines (31/0.72/4 percent)	*oppas* (noun, plural), *oppan, oppa-pout-wiggle, oppa-dongs(a)eng, oppa(-)deul, oppaoppa, oppanim, oppaneun, OppaKorea, oppaaaaaa, oppa-defense*
PC bang	10 (0.01)	1. the Philippines (2/0.05/20 percent) 2. Nigeria (2/0.05/20 percent) 3. Australia (1/0.02/10 percent) India (1/0.02/10 percent) Singapore (1/0.02/10 percent)	*PC bangs* (noun, plural)
samgyeopsal	17 (0.01)	1. the Philippines (7/0.16/41 percent) 2. Malaysia (3/0.07/18 percent) 3. Singapore (2/0.05/12 percent)	-
skinship	73 (0.04)	1. Singapore (58/1.35/79 percent) 2. Malaysia (5/0.12/7 percent) 3. the Philippines (3/0.07/4 percent)	*skinships* (noun, plural)
Tang Soo Do	25 (0.01)	1. Great Britain (13/0.03/52 percent) 2. United States (11/0.03/44 percent) 3. New Zealand (1/0.01/4 percent)	-

a total frequency of three). The item with the highest frequency (n = 772) is the address term *oppa* (which traditionally is used by younger women to address male interactants who are older than themselves but as a Korean loanword in English also has the meaning of "[a]n attractive South Korean man, esp. a famous or popular actor or singer"; OED, n.d. 'oppa'; cf. also Section 5).

As the last column shows, even in the older GloWbE data, some of the Korean items were used following English morphological rules, showing integration into the matrix language. This can be seen in the pluralization of nouns by adding the suffix *-s*, as found, for example, in *banchans*, *noonas*, *oppas*, *manhwas*, *hanboks*, and *PC bangs*. *Agyeos* is a particularly interesting case as it first undergoes conversion (from adjective to verb) to be then fitted with a third person present tense indicative suffix *-s* (see [1] and [2]). All three of these cases stem from the Singapore component (from two different web addresses) and seem to be thematically related to Korean dramas.

(1) Soo Yeon **aegyos** him and puts her head on his shoulder. (GloWbE, Singapore: General)[34]

(2) She's more disappointed in Tae-joon than Hanna who **aegyos**, Don't be so hard on Oppa! (GloWbE, Singapore: General)

In a few cases, we find Korean morphological marking used on the loanword, for example, *-deul*, the Korean plural marker, on *oppadeul* (see [3] where this refers to the members of a K-pop boyband), *-neun*, the Korean topic marker on *oppaneun* (see [4] where this is part of a lengthy explanation of the Korean lyrics in Psy's hit song *Gangnam Style*), and *-nim*, a Korean honorific suffix (roughly translatable as 'Mr./Mrs./Ms.') on *oppanim* (for an overview of the Korean morphological system and general information on Korean language structures, see Yeon & Brown, 2011).

(3) I'm speechless Ya! why they were / are very very unfair with **oppadeul**??? (GloWbE, Malaysia: General)

(4) In Korean colloquialism, "??????? (Oppan Gangnam style)" may be translated as "I love the Gangnam style" or literally translated as "Your big brother is Gangnam Style". The Korean word?? (oppa) means "a female's elder brother" but can be also used as a first-, second- or third-person masculine pronoun to designate a male who is elder or older than a female. Based on more recent cultural norms, the term has typically been used to refer to a boyfriend or male spouse. It is used as a first-person pronoun in this phrase.?? (oppan) is an abbreviation of??? (**oppaneun**).? is a topic marker, which in this case means the implied subject of the sentence is the singer

---

[34] All emphases in these and the following examples have been added. Spelling has been retained as found in the corpus. Identifiers are taken from GloWbE and NOW respectively. The country codes in the NOW identifiers can be resolved as follows: CA = Canada, IE = Ireland, IN = India, NG = Nigeria, US = United States of America.

(??). The verb "to be" is omitted, as is often the case in such short Korean sentences. Thus the literal translation of "Oppan Gangnam style" is "Your big brother is Gangnam Style". (GloWbE, Malaysia: Blog)[35]

Example (4) is an interesting example of a meta-linguistic discussion of Korean language lyrics (presumably written by a non-Korean), and appeared on the blog section of a plastic surgery clinic in Malaysia (which also discussed the singer's look and hypothesized on previous plastic surgery procedures). Likewise, Locher (2020) found meta-comments in her work on fan-subtitling of Korean dramas (also known as K-drama). Regarding relational work encoded in the Korean language, specifically address terms, the fan translators commonly subtitle in a way that "retains a Korean flavor [i.e., transliterating the original Korean word(s) and adding a short explanation in brackets] and over time, the audience is able to pick up some of the more common address terms" (Locher, 2020: 151). Khedun-Burgoine (2022: 278) showed that "the use of Korean words played an important role in the construction of fan identities" in K-pop fan communities (although also problematized by some community members as cultural appropriation). These specific communities of practice related to Korean pop culture (as demonstrated by Locher's work on K-drama and Khedun-Burgoine's work on K-pop) thus seem to contribute to the spread of Korean vocabulary items in English settings, particularly in the digital sphere. This demonstrates how language change can be initiated by small, purpose-driven communities, eventually reaching dimensions of use that are picked up by others and documented by institutions such as the *Oxford English Dictionary*.

Some of the items productively combine with other free and bound morphemes, often (but not always) in hyphenated form. For *aegyo*, for example, this includes free morpheme plus free morpheme compounds such as *aegyo-free*, *aegyo-light*, *aegyo-filled*, and free morpheme plus bound morpheme derivations such as *aegyo-tastic*, *aegyo-ish*, *aegyo-fied*, and *aegyo-y*; see (5) and (6) for two examples in context.

(5) There's also a good amount of **aegyo-filled** solo shots, which don't completely feel out of place but are definitely dispensable (GloWbE, United States: Blog)

(6) Sunny is not that pleasant. not that **'aegyo-ish'** too in real life. (GloWbE, Malaysia: Blog)

---

[35] While the original blog post is not available anymore, using the *Internet Archive*, we were able to reconstruct the original. The repeated use of question marks in this case are artifacts of GloWbE's data collection and display methods: in the original, we find words and phrases spelled in the Korean alphabet Hangul in their place (i.e., 오빠 강남 스타일, 오빠, 오빠, 오빠는, 는, and 오빠).

Other additional lemmas seem to be typical of computer-mediated discourse generally (see e.g., Darics, 2013), such as reduplication (e.g., *oppaoppa*) or letter repetition (e.g., *daebakkk, oppaaaaaa*). Altogether, the frequency numbers and the morphological productivity of the Korean loanwords in GloWbE suggest that these terms were already part of the lexical repertoire of specific internet spaces (often but not exclusively related to Korea-themed fandoms) at the time the corpus was collected (pre-2012).

Now, we turn to a survey of the use of the same lexical items in NOW, a monitor corpus of online news. The geographical contexts covered are the same as in GloWbE; however, the data is up-to-date (to the day before the corpus searches were conducted; i.e., several days in mid-April 2024). Additionally, the material in NOW stems from online newspapers, a more institutionalized form of writing than many of the blogs and websites covered in GloWbE (it should be noted, however, that NOW data also includes material from the comment sections underneath the online news reports).

In NOW, all items were retrievable (see Table 5), including *chimaek* and *mukbang* which were absent from GloWbE (see Table 4). This indicates that all items have made it to mainstream usage, in the sense that online news outlets report on them, using the respective Korean terminology. This may be followed by an explanation (and sometimes set apart as a foreign term using single or double quotation marks or italic formatting) (as in [7] from the *Bangalore Mirror*), or the terms might be used as in example (8) from the *Los Angeles Times*, without any further marking or explanation.

(7) Popular livestreaming platforms Douyin and Kuaishou said they would shut down accounts of people who gorge themselves on excessive levels of food, sometimes until they vomit – a viral video practice known as **"mukbang"** (NOW, 20-08-13 IN)

(8) If you spend any time on TikTok, you're familiar with the Korean corn dog – it's a **mukbang** favorite. Like its American counterpart, the hot dogs are coated in batter and fried on a stick. (NOW, 20-12-29 US)

In some cases, the whole article may be dedicated to a Korean phenomenon, such as a 2020 *New York Times* article on Korean side dishes titled "A Spread Worthy of Royalty" which led with "**Banchan**, the small dishes that often accompany a Korean meal, should be treasured in their own right" (Kim, 2020). These thematically dedicated articles often lead to a high frequency of Korean loanwords within a single article, as evidenced in excerpt (9), taken from the *New York Times* article on banchan.

(9) The key is in planning ahead. **Banchan-style** home cooking is cumulative, which is to say, you might make one or two dishes at a time and keep leftovers in the

Table 5 Korean loanwords used in NOW.

Lexical item	Frequency in NOW raw total (+ pmw)	Top 3 users in NOW (raw frequency/ frequency per million words/percent of all uses in the corpus)	Additional lemmas and combined forms in NOW
aegyo	186 (0.01)	1. the Philippines (65/0.12/35 percent) 2. Singapore (27/0.04/15 percent) 3. South Africa (7/0.01/4 percent)	*aegyo-filled, aegyos* (noun, plural), *aegyo(-)sal, aegyona, aegyo-prone, aegyo-heavy*
banchan	674 (0.04)	1. the Philippines (58/0.11/9 percent) 2. United States (374/0.05/55 percent) 3. Hong Kong (5/0.05/1 percent)	*banchans* (noun, plural), *banchan-focused, banchan-style, banchan-specific, banchan-like*
bulgogi	1,328 (0.07)	1. the Philippines (153/0.29/12 percent) 2. Singapore (115/0.18/9 percent) 3. Malaysia (48/0.12/4 percent)	*bulgogi-style, bulgogi-inspired, bulgogi-marinated, bulgogis* (noun, plural), *bulgogi-kimchi, bulgogi-stuffed, bulgogi-topped, bulgogi-spiced, bulgogi-loaded, bulgogi-like, bulgogi-flavoured*
chimaek	81 (0.00)	1. Singapore (27/0.04/33 percent) 2. Great Britain (21/0.01/26 percent) 3. Australia (11/0.01/14 percent)	-
daebak	182 (0.01)	1. the Philippines (37/0.07/20 percent) 2. Singapore (27/0.04/15 percent) 3. Nigeria (22/0.02/12 percent)	*DAEBAKTV*

Term	Frequency (percent)	Top countries	Derived forms
dongchimi	23 (0.00)	1. Singapore (4/0.01/17 percent) 2. Canada (5/0.00/22 percent) United States (5/0.00/22 percent) 3. India (2/0.00/9 percent) Great Britain (2/0.00/9 percent)	–
galbi	465 (0.02)	1. Singapore (56/0.11/12 percent) 2. Hong Kong (8/0.08/2 percent) 3. Singapore (23/0.04/5 percent)	*galbi(-)tang, galbi(-)ji(j)im, galbi-style, galbijib, galbijip, galbi-marinated*
hallyu	2,409 (0.13)	1. the Philippines (732/1.40/30 percent) 2. Singapore (506/0.77/21 percent) 3. Hong Kong (43/0.46/2 percent)	*hallyupopfest, hallyu(-)wood, hallyutalk, hallyutown, hallyupass, hallyulife, hallyucon, hallyu-related, hallyuween, hallyu-wave, hallyuscape, hallyupyo, hallyumart, hallyuhistory, hallyuent, hallyu-worthy, hallyu-rrific, hallyu-inspired, hallyu-chasing, hallyu-centered*
hanbok	988 (0.05)	1. the Philippines (142/0.27/14 percent) 2. Singapore (159/0.24/16 percent) 3. Hong Kong (16/0.17/2 percent)	*hanboks (noun, plural), hanbok-wearing, hanboknam, hanbok-style, hanbok-clad, hanbok-inspired, hanbok-like, hanbok-themed, hanbok-rental, hanbok-influenced*
japchae	221 (0.01)	1. the Philippines (59/0.11/27 percent) 2. Singapore (16 /0.02/7 percent) 3. United States (66/0.01/30 percent)	*japchaebab, japchae-bap*
kimbap	433 (0.02)	1. Singapore (90/0.14/21 percent) 2. the Philippines (72/0.14/17 percent) 3. Hong Kong (3/0.03/1 percent)	*kimbaps (noun, plural), kimbapchu*

Table 5 (cont.)

Lexical item	Frequency in NOW raw total (+ pmw)	Top 3 users in NOW (raw frequency/frequency per million words/percent of all uses in the corpus)	Additional lemmas and combined forms in NOW
manhwa	351 (0.02)	1. Singapore (25/0.04/7 percent) 2. the Philippines (21/0.04/6 percent) 3. United States (192/0.03/55 percent)	*manhwas* (noun, plural), *manhwa-style*, *manhwa-like*, *manhwa-based*, *manhwa-turned-TV*, *manhwaworld*, *manhwatop*, *manhwasor*, *manhwabang*
mukbang	803 (0.04)	1. the Philippines (104/0.20/13 percent) 2. Singapore (93/0.14/12 percent) 3. Malaysia (55/0.14/7 percent)	*mukbangs* (noun, plural), *mukbangers*, *mukbanger*, *mukbang-style*, *mukbanging* (verb), *mukbang-inspired*, *mukbang-prank*, *mukbang-friendly*, *mukbang-eating*, *mukbang-ASMR-style*
noona	259 (0.01)	1. the Philippines (58/0.11/22 percent) 2. Singapore (45/0.07/17 percent) 3. Hong Kong (2/0.02/1 percent)	*noonas* (noun, plural), *noona-brother*, *noona-dongsaeng*
oppa	1,146 (0.06)	1. the Philippines (354/0.68/31 percent) 2. Singapore (189/0.29/16 percent) 3. Malaysia (59/0.15/5 percent)	*oppas* (noun, plural), *oppa-dongs(a)eng*, *oppastar*, *oppa-sition*, *oppa-inspired*, *oppaa(a)(a)*, *oppa-land*, *oppa-slash-ahjussi*
PC bang	88 (0.00)	1. the Philippines (8/0.02/9 percent) 2. Ireland (17/0.01/19 percent) Great Britain (17/0.01/19 percent) Australia (17/0.01/19 percent) 3. United States (24/0.00/27 percent)	*PC bangs* (noun, plural)

samgyeopsal	122 (0.01)	1. the Philippines (91/0.17/75 percent) 2. Singapore (7/0.01/6 percent) 3. Hong Kong (1/0.01/1 percent)	*samgyeopsal-gui*
skinship	79 (0.00)	1. Singapore (29/0.04/37 percent) 2. the Philippines (4/0.01/5 percent) 3. Ghana (1/0.01/1 percent)	*skinships* (noun, plural)
Tang Soo Do	142 (0.01)	1. Malaysia (8/0.02/6 percent) 2. South Africa (20/0.02 /14 percent) 3. United States (48/0.01/34 percent)	-

fridge. The point is that you're amassing a store of **banchan** so that, come dinnertime, all that's left to do is steam the rice and take out your stash. Some **banchan** can be eaten as soon as you make them. But others are meant to be eaten later, stemming from historic methods of preservation. On the Korean Peninsula, food often had to be preserved, especially with salt, to last through the long, grueling winters. That's why fermentation is central to many **banchan**, like kimchi, pickles and jeotgal, or salted seafood (NOW, 20-09-28 US; emphasis added)

Besides three instances of *banchan*, this short excerpt also includes one instance of a compound (*banchan-style*), and two other food words from Korean: *kimchi* (also found in the OED) and *jeotgal* (not found in the OED). While the former (*kimchi*) is apparently assumed to be familiar to the reader and is not further explained (corresponding to its status of inclusion in the OED), the latter (*jeotgal*) is followed by a short explanation ("salted seafood").

While we found 54 lemma types (for 17-word forms) in GloWbE, this number was much higher for the NOW data, where 96 lemma types were identified (for 19-word forms). Surveying the top 3 lists of each table (and Figures 2 and 3 that include all uses, not just the top 3), we can also see that a larger range of regional contexts are represented in NOW (e.g., Ghana, which did not feature in the top 3s of GloWbE) and while Asian countries (mainly Singapore and the Philippines) still predominate the lists, other contexts can be found much more often too. This can of course be related to matters of differences in corpus (and subcorpus) size and corpus design, but it is also an important indicator that discourses featuring Korean loanwords have become more widespread and are also frequently picked up by the media.

Finally, due to the status of NOW as a monitor corpus, we can trace the use of Korean loanwords in the corpus over time. Figure 4 shows this development for our words of interest from 2010 (the earliest year available) to 2023 (the last full year for which data was available at the time of conducting the corpus queries).[36]

In general, we can observe an upward trend for the usage frequency of Korean loanwords in English online news article discourse, which corresponds with their codification in the OED and attests to the words' acceptance by actual language users and the still growing popularity of Korean culture in the Anglophone sphere. References to Korean culture can be conveniently expressed via the prefix *K-*, which we turn to next.

---

[36] Please note that due to the search syntax of NOW, this does not include the words separated by a space, i.e., *PC bang* and *Tang Soo Do*. As these were of generally low frequency (see Table 5), this was considered unproblematic for showing the general trend of temporal development.

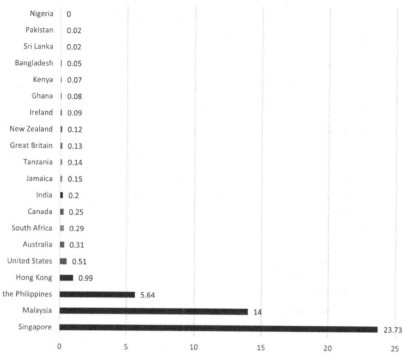

Figure 2 Frequency per million words for aegyo|banchan|bulgogi|chimaek| daebak|dongchimi|galbi|hallyu|hanbok| japchae|kimbap|manhwa|mukbang| noona|oppa|samgyeopsal|skinship in GloWbE by country.

The K-prefix

The *K*-prefix constitutes a shortening of *Korea(n)* and is found attached to nouns to designate a relationship "to South Korea and its (popular) culture" (OED, n.d. 'K-combining form'). The OED added the prefix in its 2021-update, which included many of the Korean loanwords given at the beginning of this section in Table 3. The OED lists two resulting forms, *K-pop* and *K-drama*, noting that the former is the one recorded earlier. The example attestations in the OED (earliest from 1999), however, already hint at the productivity of the prefix as we find that they contain (in addition to *K-pop* and *K-drama*) the forms *K-wave*, *K-food*, *K-beauty*, *K-culture*, and *K-style*. Khedun-Burgoine and Kiaer (2023) have recently reported on the spread of Korean culture, with the *K*-prefix representing to many an instantly recognizable shorthand for Korean cultural products of many kinds. Note that the prefix is variably written with an upper or lowercase letter (maintaining the original spelling of *Korea(n)* or disregarding it), an interesting variation, which is beyond our interest here though (our searches

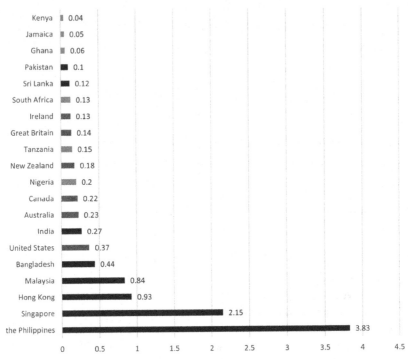

Figure 3 Frequency per million words for aegyo|banchan|bulgogi|chimaek|
daebak|dongchimi|galbi|hallyu|hanbok| japchae|kimbap|manhwa|mukbang|
noona|oppa|samgyeopsal|skinship in NOW by country.

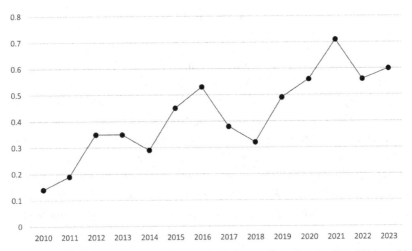

Figure 4 Frequency per million words for aegyo|banchan|bulgogi|chimaek|
daebak|dongchimi|galbi|hallyu|hanbok| japchae|kimbap|manhwa|mukbang|
noona|oppa|samgyeopsal|skinship in NOW by year.

Table 6 *K*-prefixed items in NOW occurring at least twenty times (sorted by raw frequency).

Lexical items (exact raw frequency in brackets)	Frequency range
K-pop (63,893), *K-drama* (11,617)	>10,000
K-dramas (7,165), *K-beauty* (2,081)	1,000–10,000
K-league (853), *K-town* (692), *K-rock* (614), *K-culture* (442), *K-content* (269), *K-wave* (244), *K-Water* (188), *K-fashion* (186), *K-food* (156), *K-entertainment* (105), *K-dramas/films* (100)	100–999
K-variety (*show/s*) (98), *K-music* (92), *K-pop-inspired* (71), *K-hip-hop* (69), *K-movie* (68), *K-idols* (67), *K-hip* (*hop*) (59), *K-dramaland* (59), *K-indie* (44), *K-idol* (42), *K-global* (42), *K-fans* (41), *K-movies* (38), *K-celebs* (37), *K-media* (34), *K-horror* (33), *K-pops* (31), *K-actress* (29), *K-bbq* (29), *K-exim* (29), *K-film* (29), *K-films* (29), *K-pop-related* (28), *K-r&b* (28), *K-video* (28), *K-city* (26), *K-netizens* (26), *K-quarantine* (26), *K-romance* (25), *K-festa* (24), *K-actor* (24), *K-contents* (24), *K-dance* (23), *K-tigers* (21), *K-con* (21), *K-industry* (21), *K-box* (20), *K-zombie* (20), *K-reality* (20)	20–99

included both upper and lowercase spelling and do not differentiate between the two; all instances given here are spelled with an uppercase <K>).

Searching for *K*-prefixed items in NOW returns 233,486 tokens and 4,107 types. This of course subsumes numerous items which begin with *k-*/*K-* but are unrelated to the Korean context (e.g., *K-12* [from kindergarten to grade 12] n = 43,498; *K-9* [reference to police dogs; cf. canine] n = 14,891). We therefore manually examined up to the first twenty concordance lines of each *K*-prefixed word that occurred more than twenty times in NOW to determine whether the word was an item of interest (with the *K*-standing in for *Korea* or *Korean*) or not.[37] For instance, while *K-Stew* (n = 208) could conceivably index a Korean food item, this is instead a reference to the US-American actress Kristen Stewart. Of the 370 types with a frequency of at least 20, 54 types thus remained, which we sorted into Table 6 (all numbers from mid-April 2024).

---

[37] This is of course prone to some error, as for example, the first twenty concordance lines for *K-car* attest to a non-target use (i.e., a car produced by Chrysler), but later concordance lines might reveal occasional use of *K-car* to refer to a Korean car. However, due to the high volume of hits, the described procedure was adopted as both feasible and revealing the items which had a clear relation to the Korean context.

In addition to the items listed in Table 6, which were predominantly relatable to our target *K*-prefix, a number of other words showed a range of alternative uses alongside clear usages of the target prefix, attesting to the multiple semantic resolutions of *K*-, which can also stand, for example, for *Kasikorn* in *K-Bank* (a Thai bank) or for *Kakatiya* in *K-hub* (which references the *Kakatiya University Entrepreneurship, Incubation and Career Hubs*). These items further subsume, for example, *K-series* (which can refer to Korean TV series or a Honda car series), *K-love* (which references either a TV series related to Korea from the Philippines or a US-American Christian radio station), and *K-dog* (which can refer to a Korean-style hot dog but also has various other uses as a nickname for people and animals). The full list of these items with multiple semantic resolution is: *K-series* (n = 1,365), *K-love* (n = 230), *K-star* (n = 191), *K-style* (n = 101), *K-factor* (n = 99), *K-sports* (n = 98), *K-band* (n = 83), *K-startup* (n = 79), *K-team* (n = 52), *K-plus* (n = 39), *K-pub* (n = 33), *K-girls* (n = 31), *K-stars* (n = 29), *K-group* (n = 28), *K-dog* (n = 25), *K-hub* (n = 24), *K-serials* (n = 24), *K-community* (n = 23), *K-bank* (n = 21), and *K-glass* (n = 21).

As Table 6 and this list demonstrate, many *K*-words can be related to phenomena of Korean pop culture, among them the items with the highest frequencies of use, namely, *K-pop* and *K-drama/s*, but also lower frequency items such as *K-music*, *K-entertainment*, *K-actor*, and *K-romance*. We also find *K-* used to index the inherent Korean-ness of events (such as *K-con*, *K-Global*, or *K-Festa*), companies (e.g., *K-Water*), and food items (*K-dog*, *K-bbq*, *K-food*). This also extends to the branding of more abstract concepts or procedures, such as the Korean form of quarantining during the Covid-19 pandemic, see (10).

(10)   The South Korean economy was one of the least affected by the pandemic. The government was so proud of its success in fighting infections that it coined a name for it: **K-Quarantine**. (NOW, 21-07-28 US)

In some cases, *K*-terms can be found clustered together in very close proximity. This is demonstrated in examples (11) and (12) and can evoke negative connotations of 'flooding' or 'excess' (see, e.g. [12]), where the text continues to describe these phenomena as "a global popular-culture invasion" by South Korea.

(11)   And it's not only **K-beauty** but **K-food, K-pop, K-drama** have also gained traction in India. (NOW, 24-01-05 NG)
(12)   Whether it's **K-pop, K-dramas, K-movies, K-beauty, K-games**, or **K-reality**, they're part of a global popular-culture invasion by a South Korea that is about one third larger than Tasmania but with 100 times the Apple Isle's population density. (NOW, 23-03-31 AU)

This clustering seems to facilitate creative uses of the *K*-prefix, as done in example (13) from a 2024 article in the Indian newspaper *The Economic Times*, which not only uses the well-known and OED-listed *K-pop* and *K-dramas* but also *K-colleges*, *K-noodles*, and *K-ool*, a creative (but maybe somewhat strenuous) play on the word *cool*.

(13) **K-colleges** may well be the latest addition to the list of **K-ool** things comprising **K-pop**, **K-dramas** and **K-noodles**, with Indian students increasingly considering South Korea for higher education, according to consultants. (NOW, 24-03-24 IN)

Indeed, looking for collocates (+/-4) of *K-pop* (as the *K*-item with the highest frequency in NOW) that also begin with *K*- returns 1,650 instances in NOW. The eighty-four different *K*-collocate types include high-frequency items, such as *K-pop* itself (n = 504), but also lower- and low-frequency items, including *K-beau*, *K-diplomacy*, *K-language* (*school*), and *K-hole* ("... delve into the **K-pop K-hole**"; NOW, 17-11-24 US). A clear reference to K-pop (or the *K*-prefix in general of course) seems to license the ad hoc coinage of new *K*-items, as we have also done in this section, for example, in 'K-collocate' and 'K-word.' The transparency of *K*-prefixation is aptly demonstrated in example (14), which expands on the use of the prefix (i.e., "things with 'K' stuck on them") and the global Korean Wave.

(14) Aware of the growing global popularity of **K-content**, led by multiple Oscar winner *Parasite* and Netflix's global phenomenon *Squid Game*, Lee says BIFF organisers nevertheless have no thought of leaning into this new and stronger wave of popularity.

"We are being very careful about [words like] '**K-culture**' and '**K-contents**' and things with '**K**' stuck on them," says Lee. (NOW, 22-10-04 IE)

Last but not least, as can already be seen in Table 6, at least one *K*-item has become itself a productive base for further word formation processes: *K-pop* (see *K-pop-inspired* in Table 6). Searching for different word forms of *K-pop* in NOW returns eighty-nine different types. Many of these, among them *K-pop-inspired* (n = 71), are the result of compounding. Other examples include *K-pop-related* (n = 28), *K-pop-idol-turned-actor* (n = 8), *K-pop-fandom* (n = 2), and *K-pop-stanning* (n = 1). In addition, *K-pop* also serves as basis for derivation, as demonstrated by items like *K-popper* (n = 13), *K-pop-esque* (n = 5), *K-pop-y* (n = 3), and *K-pop-ish* (n = 2). As we can see in examples (15) and (16), it is also occasionally used as a verb or participle, with *K-popping* occurring five times and *K-popped* twice in NOW.

(15) "Whereas our cheerleaders are sort of **K-popped** out," my friend texted me. (NOW, 18-02-08 US)

(16) I mean, it's just dance, dance, dance. They are **K-Popping** fools. (NOW, 18-02-09 CA)

While not exclusively relatable to the Korean context, the *K*-prefix has become iconic for its indexing of Korean-ness and has certainly caught on in the branding of products as being from or related to South Korea. The K-branding strategy is not only amply used by companies but also openly embraced by the Korean government, as can be seen, for example, in the governmental *K-move* campaign, an overseas employment training program for Korean youths (see HRDK, n.d.). This fits in with the Korean government's endeavors to support the K-pop industry in recognition of the economic potential it holds for the country. As one of the latest instantiations, this involved the announcement that a visa for K-pop fans will be introduced in 2024: The Hallyu or K-culture training visa (Kelleher, 2024). Word formation with *K*- has truly become embraced by South Korean actors and beyond; and as former first lady of South Korea Kim Jung-sook stated in a press release: "We feel proud of our Koreanness when we see words with that added 'K-'" (quoted in Dunbar, 2023: n.p.).

Conclusion

From *kimchi* to *mukbang*, Korean loanwords in English constitute part of the mutual influences between English and Korean in dynamic and thriving contact settings, not only in South Korea and the USA but also across English varieties around the world. Riding to a certain degree on the 'Korean Wave' and the global success of Korean pop cultural products, Korean words have made a sustained impact on the English lexicon, as also observed in institutionalized form in the *Oxford English Dictionary*. In this section, we used the *Global Web-based English Corpus* (GloWbE) and the *News on the Web Corpus* (NOW) to reveal usage frequencies and productivity of word-formation patterns related to Korean lexis used in English writing, which in the future could be supplemented with spoken language observations. The *K*-prefix, in particular, has become a truly transnational phenomenon, clearly indexing Korean-ness in South Korea and throughout the English-speaking sphere – from Singapore and Philippine English to American and British English and beyond. To what extent the *K*-prefix has made inroads in other languages (such as German, Chinese, or Japanese) remains to be investigated.

5 Korean Cultural Exports: From K-Pop to Mukbang

Introduction

South Korea's global appeal currently rests to a large degree on the proliferation of Korean pop culture products around the world. This includes, among others, music, TV shows and movies, fashion, and food. In this section, we take a closer look at the stellar success of Korean culture exports (i.e., the Korean Wave, *hallyu*) and their relationship to matters of language. K-pop lyrics, as we show in a small corpus-based study, abundantly and creatively draw on both Korean and English as essential linguistic resources for global success. We also discuss the use of language by K-pop fans. In the second part of the section, we turn to the delectable matter of food in (1) general food-themed videos and (2) mukbang (i.e., performances of eating), which has evolved into the global genre of 'eating shows.' Our English-language instantiations of mukbang, that is, eating shows, abundantly draw on references to Korean culture and language in order to establish their grounding in the mukbang tradition. This occurs via code-switches (both in the videos themselves and their textual descriptions) but also the consumption of Korean food items and explicit references to Korean culture, society, and alimentary traditions. Korea's cultural exports thus contribute to the further entanglement of Korean and English.

Hallyu, the Korean Cultural Wave

Korean cultural exports became so popular that they were designated with their own term, *hallyu* (한류), the Korean Wave (a word by now so firmly entrenched in English that it can be found in the *Oxford English Dictionary*; see Section 4). The origins of hallyu can be traced to the mid-1990s onwards, when Korean TV dramas and popular music gained popularity in other Asian countries such as China and Japan. From there, fan bases developed beyond Asia, including South America, the Middle East, and Europe (see the contributions in Marinescu, 2014). Moreover, the dissemination of all things Korean is assured via social media, from YouTube to online chatting (see, e.g., Lee & Nornes, 2015; Jin, Yoon & Min, 2021).

While Korean TV dramas and music might well have ignited the spark for an interest in Korean culture, hallyu extends far beyond TV and music at this point in time. Individuals who develop an interest in Korea may not necessarily be initiated into Korean culture via K-pop or TV dramas – their interest may indeed be based on using Korean skincare products, developing a friendship with a Korean student who is studying outside Korea, or rooting for the Korean footballer Son Heung-min, who plays for Tottenham Hotspur. The popularity of Korean food is yet another example of how Korean culture, beyond K-drama, has spread (see the later discussion on food, restaurants, and mukbang). As a final example for the reach of Korean culture we refer to reports on multiple overseas orders placed for the traditional Korean clothing known as *hanbok*, after BTS singer Jungkook was seen shopping for such an outfit (Gibson, 2020).

As a consequence of this widespread cultural interest, hallyu has also contributed to an increase in people learning Korean (see Section 1) as well as an increase in Korea-bound tourism (see Lee & How, 2021). In fact, according to *GoWithGuide* (2024: n.p.), "over 17.5 million visitors arrived in South Korea in 2019, which is 14% higher than the previous year."[38] Ultimately, hallyu can be considered to have profound linguistic impact as individuals with an interest in Korea may find themselves becoming more acquainted with the language, seen with the inclusion of Korean words in the OED (see Section 4), or indeed learning the language in preparation for a visit to Korea, or to connect with the global community of K-pop or K-drama fans (see Khedun-Burgoine, 2022; Locher, 2020).

Lee (2008: 175) describes hallyu as "a highly complex and multi-layered formation that is composed of real, imagined, and hybrid cultural practices, a diverse range of lived experiences, and sets of powerful discourses which exist at national, translocal, and transnational levels." This quote captures the scope of hallyu, at once a national phenomenon, yet clearly extending to a global audience. Furthermore, the reference to hybridity in the quote can be seen in how Korean culture has been appropriated by non-Koreans, or perhaps interpreted, as we will exemplify shortly. Nye (2004) discusses soft power, explaining that such "rests on the ability to shape the preferences of others" (4), also referring to it succinctly as "attractive power" (6), which we can apply to the Korean context. Overall, there is clearly an attraction toward Korea for many that accompanies their viewing of Korean dramas, such as the recently acclaimed *Squid Game*, or following their favorite K-pop singers or, indeed, learning the language for a hoped-for future in Korea. The attraction can further be seen on a more concrete level, involving, for example, the physically attractive leads seen in Korean TV dramas or within the realm of K-pop, which often further contributes to the popularity of these pop culture products around the world. With both Korean and Korean English (as well as other varieties of English; see Lee, 2007, 2011b) being used, for instance, in K-pop, K-pop (and K-culture) fans around the world then use and change Korean and Korean English, with innovations at times extending beyond the K-pop and K-culture sphere. An example for this can be found in how the Korean word *oppa* is now used by K-pop fans to refer to an attractive, young male singer, an example of the aforementioned hybridity of hallyu, in which a Korean word has been appropriated by non-Koreans and undergone semantic shift as a result (see Ahn, 2019). The 2021 K-update by the OED (see Section 4) has added *oppa* to the dictionary, including both the original Korean sense (i.e., "a girl's or woman's elder brother. Also as a respectful form of address or term of

---

[38] Tourism experienced a sharp decline due to the Covid-19 pandemic (2020–2022), but 2023 saw the tourism sector recover to 11.03 million annual visitors (Statista, 2024).

endearment, and in extended use with reference to an older male friend or boyfriend") as well as the 'new' English sense (i.e., "An attractive South Korean man, esp. a famous or popular actor or singer") (see OED, n.d. 'oppa').

A further means to understand the global proliferation of Korean culture is based on the spread of concrete manifestations of Korean culture per se. For example, the second author lives in Manchester, having arrived in 2002. At that time, there was just one Korean restaurant – *Koreana* – which opened in 1985, as well as a Korean snack shop. But conducting an internet search for Korean restaurants in Manchester in 2024, nine venues come up (e.g., *Koreana, Ban di Bul*, and *Annyeong*). Some might be more fast food oriented or takeaway establishments, but all nonetheless clearly serve Korean food. Moreover, recently the Korean grocery store chain *Oseyo* opened in Manchester, selling all manner of Korean goods, from green tea to children's snacks. *Oseyo* is the largest UK retailer of Korean goods, with the Manchester branch its eleventh store opening in the UK (Pellant, 2023). Even more recently, *KSTARS* opened in Manchester, selling K-pop merchandise. From the example of this one city alone, we can thus see how, over a twenty-year period, Korean culture – including food, K-pop merchandise, *noraebang* (karaoke), Korean beauty products, and even Korean classes at the University of Manchester – has become more prominent.

The spread of Korean culinary culture does not only meet the demands for this particular cuisine but also involves Korean culture indirectly. In some places, Korean masks are placed on the restaurant walls and Korean music – traditional and K-pop – is played. Restaurant names themselves also contribute to the spread of culture through language. For example, 안녕 (*annyeong*), of the eponymous restaurant in Manchester, is an informal way to greet people in Korea. The London-based Korean restaurant *Arirang* owes its name to a famous Korean folk song (아리랑), with the song popular in both North and South Korea and included as part of Korea's intangible cultural assets by the *South Korean Cultural Heritage Administration*. Though these examples might seem negligible to some, in as much as many restaurant patrons may not consider the cultural relevance or significance of the name of the establishment, they nonetheless can act for some as a means to engage with the culture more fully.

We will delve further into the culinary world of Korea shortly, but we hope that the discussion so far has shown that it would be somewhat superficial to rest one's understanding of hallyu on Korean music and drama alone, though this has mostly been the instigator for the Korean cultural wave as we know it. It is also entirely plausible that someone has a keen passion for Korean culture, which does not extend to Korean pop culture at all but instead rests on classic literature, architecture, and the likes. Recently, Gibson (2020) has discussed how the soft power of Korea has started to involve Korean celebrities' involvement within diplomatic events and political negotiations, thus putting a literal face on the subject. Gibson cautions Korea, however, as to how it might best apply such instances of its soft power, explaining that "anything South Korean stars do or say—such as waving a Taiwanese flag, supporting Korean claims to islands also claimed by Japan, or even just honoring South Korean and American sacrifices during the Korean War—can turn into foreign policy disputes" (2020: n.p.). This is something for the Korean government, which has started to draw extensively on the power of K-culture for economic gain of the country (see Section 4), to perhaps consider for the foreseeable future. For the remaining section, however, we want to have a closer look at K-pop and K-food (as instantiated by online food displays and mukbang).

K-Pop

Until the 1990s, no, or hardly any, English was used in Korean music (Lee, 2004: 429),[39] which contrasts strongly with the abundance of English within the Korean music sphere in more recent years, as attested at a qualitative level in the works by Lee (2004, 2007, 2011b) and Lawrence (2010). A pilot type study by Rüdiger 2021a on twenty high-performing K-pop songs in 2018 found that roughly a fourth of the 4,188 tokens examined were in English. Previous research has also shown that the Englishes featured in K-pop songs range from standard varieties of English to African American English (cf. Lee, 2004, 2007) and forms of Korean English (cf. Lawrence, 2010; Rüdiger, 2021a). In order to systematically identify the level of English use in contemporary K-pop lyrics (including small-scale diachronic changes) and to illustrate such usage, we compiled the *Music Bank Corpus* (MBC). *Music Bank*[40] is a South Korean weekly TV music program (broadcast on *KBS2* and *KBS World*), which as part of its programming features a countdown chart of K-pop songs, namely *K-Charts*. Currently, the order of songs in *K-Charts* is determined by a mixture of digital music charts, album sales, broadcast frequency on KBS, fan voting via an app, and social media charts (see Wikipedia, n.d. 'Music Bank (TV program)'). To construct the *Music Bank Corpus*, we sampled the lyrics of all weekly winners (i.e., the most popular songs) from four entire years, that is, 2023 (the most current year which was complete at the time of writing) and then moving back in time in five-year steps to 2018, 2013, and

---

[39] This can certainly be related to the ban of "songs with more than one third of their lyrics in English . . . by the semi-state Korean Public Performance Ethics Committee" (Jin & Ryoo, 2014: 121) which was in effect until the mid-1990s.

[40] In the Korean original: 뮤직뱅크.

2008. As the same song can win in consecutive weeks and each song was only sampled once, the number of winning songs per year is less than 52.[41] The official lyrics for each song (including chorus) were then extracted online and processed for further corpus analysis with AntConc (Anthony, 2023). We then automatically annotated each lyric file for the use of either Hangul or the English alphabet, which allows us to analyze the language use in K-pop songs. It should be kept in mind, however, that this procedure, while very effective, does not allow us to identify English words spelled using Hangul (which could be either established, codified loanwords or nonce-borrowings; see Section 3).[42] It also relies on the written lyrics instead of an auditory analysis of the way the songs are actually sung. Nevertheless, it provides us with reliable numbers of overall English usage in K-pop songs – with the investigation of pronunciation in K-pop songs, for instance, as a research desideratum for the future.

Altogether, the MBC covers 146 songs and nearly 40,000 words (see Table 7). We can see how English use in 2008 and 2013 is relatively similar (33.17 and 29.04 English words per hundred words [phw]; 82 and 77 English words per song on average),[43] and we can observe this increasing notably by 2018 (39.82 phw and 120 English words per song on average) and even further by 2023 (59.93 phw and 198 English words per song on average). Interestingly, even though there are a (low) number of songs entirely in Korean in 2008 and 2013, only one can be found in 2018, and this number drops to zero in 2023. 2023 is also the first year in the MBC to feature a song entirely in English. Despite the rise of English usage in K-pop, there seems to be an unspoken exigency to avoid songs featuring only one language – that is, successful K-pop songs usually feature both English and Korean, with English taking larger and larger parts of this proportion. Linguistic hybridity (i.e., using both Korean and English) in K-pop can indeed be likened to a "commercial imperative" (Jin & Ryoo, 2014: 129), as K-pop relies on Korean–English entanglements to appeal

---

[41] The list of winning songs for each year can be found at https://en.wikipedia.org/wiki/ List_of_Music_Bank_Chart_winners_(2008), https://en.wikipedia.org/wiki/List_of_Music_ Bank_Chart_winners_(2013), https://en.wikipedia.org/wiki/List_of_Music_Bank_ Chart_winners_(2018), and https://en.wikipedia.org/wiki/List_of_Music_Bank_Chart_ winners_(2023).

[42] There is of course the possibility to use the English alphabet to write non-English words. This was encountered prominently only in one song (from the 2023 data), namely *Baila Conmigo* (by ONEUS), which featured altogether 37 Spanish words (which were excluded from the analysis of English language use in the MBC presented here). Manual checking of the corpus files revealed no significant use of other languages spelled in English (besides English). No other scripts were found in the data.

[43] There is a small dip in numbers when comparing 2008 to 2013; extending the MBC to cover more years might be helpful in finding an explanation for this. Nevertheless, the difference is small, in particular when comparing it to the rise in numbers in the last two corpus segments.

Table 7 English usage in the *Music Bank Corpus*.

	2008	2013	2018	2023
# of songs	21	36	37	42
Types //	1,696 //	2,743 //	2,872 //	3,153 //
tokens (overall)	5,215	9,457	11,191	13,895
English types // English tokens	221 // 1,730	272 // 2,772	458 // 4,456	895 // 8,327
English words per 100 words	33.17	29.04	39.82	59.93
English words per song on average	82	77	120	198
percent of top 100 words which are English	46 percent	43 percent	58 percent	80 percent
# of songs completely in English	0	0	0	1
# of songs completely in Korean	2	5	1	0

to a global audience. A particularly interesting case in point here concerns K-pop boyband sensation BTS, which in a move to rebrand announced in 2017 that the acronym *BTS* which originally was resolved as Korean 방탄소년단 (*bangtan sonyeondan*; lit. 'Bulletproof Boyscouts'), now could also be read as **B**eyond the **S**cene (see Wikipedia, n.d. 'BTS'), a full name which is much less opaque to an international audience than the original.

As part of the corpus analysis, we extracted the top 100 words (in terms of frequency) of each subcorpus, with 80 percent of the 100 most frequent words in 2023 indeed being English (up from 46 percent and 43 percent in 2008 and 2013). Looking more closely at the top five words from each year (see Table 8), we find that (1) English predominates at the top of these word lists as well, and (2) English usage involves function words (like the pronouns *I, you, it,* and *me*), lexical words (like the noun *girl*, the verb *tell*), and vocalizations (like *oh*). While vocalizations by themselves cannot be categorized as being English or Korean (or necessarily any other language), the lyric composers decided to spell them in English (<oh>) instead of Korean (<오>) and for that reason they were retained for our analysis.[44]

The inclusion of English in K-pop lyrics can range from entire segments in English, as illustrated in (1), code-switching in-between segments as demonstrated

---

[44] And in fact, we can find numerous instances of vocalizations spelled in Korean in the MBC, which means that lyric composers do draw on both spelling systems for their representation.

Table 8 Top five words in the *Music Bank Corpus* across subcomponents.

	2008	**2013**	**2018**	**2023**
1	*I*	*oh*	*oh*	*I*
2	*you*	*I*	*yeah*	*you*
3	*tell*	*it*	*you*	*it*
4	*baby*	*me*	*I*	*me*
5	*girl*	내 (*nae*, 'my')	내 (*nae*, 'my')	*oh*

in (2), and single word code-switches. The latter is demonstrated in examples (3) (matrix language English, single word switch to Korean) and (4) (matrix language Korean, single word switch to English).

(1) Baby, you're my trampoline
     You make me bounce (Cho Yong-pil_Bounce_2013)[45]

(2) 아픈 건 없어지겠지만 상처들은 영원해
     But that's why it's called beautiful pain (BtoB_Beatiful Pain_2018)
     [The pain will disappear but the scars are forever – But that's why it's called beautiful pain][46]

(3) I don't want to
     Walk in this 미로 (New Jeans_Ditto_2023)
     [I don't want to – Walk in this maze]

(4) 지금 push 내 버튼을 켜줘 (Wanna One_Light_2018)
     [Push right now, turn my button on]

Interestingly, the Korean word 미로 (*miro*, 'maze') in (3) does not carry the Korean locative marker -에 (*-e*) that would usually be obligatory in this context. There are, however, multiple cases where the English words carry Korean particles. For instance, in (5), the English noun *party* carries the aforementioned locative marker -에 (*-e*), and in (6), the focus marker -은 (*-eun*) is attached to *volume*.

(5) 이 party에 준비된 blue champagne (G(I)-dle_Queencard_2023)
     [Blue champagne prepared for this party]

(6) 가녀린 몸매 속 가려진 volume은 두 배로 (Blackpink_Ddu-Du Ddu-Du_2018)
     [Thin body frames with hidden volume twice as much]

---

[45] We provide the English titles of the songs and artists to avoid additional translations. For an analysis of English use in song titles and artist names in K-pop, see Rüdiger (2021b).

[46] For reasons of space, we provide English translations of the Korean song lyrics but no transliteration. Original English in the songs is underlined in the translations.

We also find a number of nonstandard English forms in our K-pop lyrics corpus, such as double superlative marking on an adjective in (7), minus-indefinite articles in (8), (9), and (10), minus-auxiliaries in (7) and (10), and a minus-preposition in the multi-word verb construction *get out of* in (11).

(7)　누나도 알지 You the bestest (G.NA_Oops!_2013)
　　　[Nuna, you know you're the bestest right?]
(8)　I'm walkin' like zombie uh (Monsta X_Shoot Out_2018)
(9)　It's one way road to you (Tempest_Vroom Vroom_2023)
(10)　You waiting long long time (McMong_Circus_2008)
(11)　Tired of all your lies and excuses now just get out my face (Ailee_U&I_2013)

While some of these nonstandard forms can be related to stylistic reasons (e.g., "bestest") or potentially occur due to rhythm and rhyme, some of them, like the minus-indefinite articles, minus-prepositions, and minus-auxiliaries have been attested in previous research on Korean English morpho-syntax (see Section 2).

Accordingly, Khedun-Burgoine and Kiaer (2023) discuss K-pop in terms of how it has not only disseminated the Korean language and culture but also how it has helped to spread forms of Korean English. Their research shows how K-pop fans from all over the world are bonding not only via music but also particular forms of language use, which can also be found codified in lay online dictionaries, glossaries, and blogs that we will see throughout this section. Such fandom language is used and understood worldwide, often shared through social media, so that a K-pop fan in Algeria can 'speak,' or type, in the same way as a fan in Brazil. Lee and Jin (2019: 429) report that "global youth, from the US to Chile, chant for K-pop" and this also reflects the fandom language used (which we would like to point out is not a phenomenon exclusively related to K-pop; cf. the idea of a 'fanilect' mentioned in connection to Taylor Swift, see Mair, 2023). We already gave an example for this, namely, the Korean word *oppa* (오빠; 'older brother' [used by female speakers]), which underwent semantic shift in the K-pop fanilect (which as mentioned previously found its way into the OED). A similar kind of semantic shift – from age-specific address term to nonage-specific address term – has also been observed for the corresponding female form, *eonni* (언니; 'older sister' [used by female speakers]) (Ahn, 2019; Khedun-Burgoine, 2022; Khedun-Burgoine & Kiaer, 2023). Specific Korean cultural concepts, such as 'skinship' which refers to "intimate physical contact between two individuals, involving a range of behaviours such as hand holding, hugging, and caressing" (Khedun-Burgoine, 2022: 214), have taken on special significance in K-pop communities and have become resemiotized as part of 'shipping'[47] culture (see Khedun-Burgoine, 2022: Chapter 7).

Furthermore, Baratta (2021) reports on additional examples of English words having undergone semantic shift and being used in K-pop fan communities. These include items such as *all-kill* and *bias* (see [12] and [13] for two examples from recent forum threads on *Hallyu+*, a K-pop community platform); respectively, these refer to a Korean song going to number one on all the Korean music charts, and the preference a K-pop fan has for a particular band member (e.g., *he's my bias*).

(12) DAY6 have achieved a Perfect **All-Kill** with "HAPPY"[48]

(13) If you were to give each member of your **bias** group a CF[49] of your choice what would it be?[50]

Combined, then, the examples thus far – whether based on Korean or English lexis – have taken on new meaning and are used among knowing K-pop fans worldwide. We can see this reaching far beyond US-American and British contexts. Touhami and Al-Haq (2017), for instance, discuss Korean fanbases in Algeria, who have adopted, as with other fans perhaps, Korean pronunciation for certain words. Thus, *coffee* and *pizza* might be realized, in specific contexts of course, more as *cop-pee* and *pija*. There are additional web-based resources dedicated to K-pop English (such as Richelle, 2016; Morin, 2019; Pham, 2020), demonstrating that there is a lexical usage that exists among fans, hence a means to codify it via online resources. There we can find lay definitions of lexical items considered of particular importance for K-fan communities, as demonstrated in (14) and (15) for *maknae* and *killing point*.

(14) **Maknae**

A Maknae is a person who is youngest in a particular group of people. For example, Mark may have been the Maknae in NCTU but is no longer the Maknae in NCT127 as Haechan is younger than him. (Richelle, 2016: n.p.)

(15) **Killing Point**

The moment in a choreography, song, or performance that is considered the most dramatic or best part. (Morin, 2019: n.p.)

---

[47] *Shipping* is a term used in many fandom cultures and refers to a desire to see a romantic relationship evolve between characters (e.g., Mulder and Scully in *X-Files*) or real-life people (e.g., members of a pop group).

[48] https://hallyuplus.net/threads/day6-have-achieved-a-perfect-all-kill-with-happy.82555/.

[49] *CF* is the acronym of 'commercial film.'

[50] https://hallyuplus.net/threads/if-you-were-to-give-each-member-of-your-bias-group-a-cf-of-your-choice-what-would-it-be.82612/.

This can be taken as further evidence for a fan-based language disseminated – and codified – on fan-made online outlets, such as forums and discussion and message boards, intersecting of course with a wider interest in K-culture products (see also Locher, 2020; Khedun-Burgoine, 2022).

Altogether, this has shown how language use in K-pop and language use by K-pop fan communities embody the transnational aspects of Korean Englishes. Both of these are characterized by intense code-switching, localized forms of Korean Englishes, semantic shift, and linguistic creativity. The transnational aspects involved with Korean Englishes, those which go beyond the borders of both Korea and English-speaking countries, are realized with K-pop fans who, indeed, are neither L1 speakers of Korean or English. Thus, an Arabic-speaking Algerian, who may well speak English, can also use Korean English when required, and in this case a variety tied to K-pop. The implication of this is that Korean Englishes are being used internationally and by non-Koreans in the first instance. Indeed, Korea now has a large number of foreigners residing in the country,[51] notably in Seoul, and so is perhaps not as homogenous as it once was; this might also produce different varieties of English in Korea – a development yet to be surveyed by systematic linguistic research. In the final part of this section, we move on to a focus on K-culture products, as instantiated by Korean food.

K-Food

This part discusses the various ways in which Korean culinary culture and food-related phenomena have become popular around the world. We already briefly noted the global mark left by Korean cuisine in the restaurant sphere earlier in this section, but we now want to first address online Korean food displays in short and then mukbang (an originally Korean genre of online eating) in more detail.

Online Korean Food Displays

Koreans and non-Koreans have contributed to making Korean cooking, foods, and foodways globally visible, both in the home kitchen and in public dining spaces. Maangchi, for instance, has been teaching the world how to cook Korean dishes with her YouTube channel,[52] which she created in 2007, and website.[53] Her extraordinary success is reflected in the number of subscribers her YouTube channel has reached (6.4 million in June 2024) and her publishing

---

[51] According to the Hankyoreh website (2024), as of late 2023, there were 2.51 million foreigners residing in Korea (roughly 5 percent of the overall population).

[52] www.youtube.com/@Maangchi.   [53] www.maangchi.com/.

two well-received cookbooks (*Maangchi's Real Korean Cooking* and *Maangchi's Big Book of Korean Cooking*). Importantly, Maangchi always stresses the Korean names for dishes (and at times ingredients) and often explains their cultural, societal, and personal significance which contributes to a bid for cultural authenticity in her cooking (see Sprague, 2024). Maangchi, dubbed by the *New York Times* "YouTube's Julia Child" (Moskin, 2015: n.p.), is but one of many successful diasporic Korean online cooks, whose content can be found spread throughout platforms such as YouTube and TikTok.

Besides these instructional approaches (as in how to cook Korean food), other social media influencers draw on the Korean cuisine for entertainment purposes. A case in point is the popular YouTube channel 영국남자[54] *Korean Englishman.*[55] The videos on the channel focus on Korean culture, with food playing a large part in the shows. This often takes the form of individuals being introduced to Korean food for the first time, such as English schoolchildren for whom Korean dishes are prepared, or international celebrities trying Korean food at a restaurant. Beyond this, viewers can also see various locations within Korea and so, overall, the channel is bringing Korean culture to the public in an accessible manner, involving a respect for the culture, but also presented with a degree of cheeky humor, which contributes to the popular allure of the videos. Korean food has also found its way into other mainstream online spaces such as Reddit, where the subreddit r/KoreanFood counts more than 630,000 members (as of June 2024). As the following excerpt from a recent r/KoreanFood post shows, Korean language food terminology abounds in this online space as well (though usually written in English and not in the Korean alphabet Hangul).

> My son isn't very picky and has a great palate. He loveeeees **Tteokbokki** with sweet **Gochujang** sauce I make with cheese topped off. He loves **kimbap**, (beef) and is obsessed with **Mukbangs** 😊 We frequently have **bulgogi, chadol**, **LA Galbi** with rice, I really want to try to make some **banchan** but no idea how to even start. He loves all those, but I want him to try other things he sees on there. Any suggestions/ recipes are welcome. Thank you in advance! (emphasis added)[56]

Besides various food items, the author of the post mentioned that their 4-year-old son is "obsessed" with a type of video called *mukbang*, which we now turn to next as a cultural export from Korea which concerns a whole genre.

---

[54] *yeonggug namja.*

[55] www.youtube.com/@koreanenglishman (6.01 million subscribers as of June 2024), created by Joshua Carrott.

[56] www.reddit.com/r/KoreanFood/comments/1dbboz4/my_4_yo_loves_tteokbokki_what_are_some_other/.

Mukbang

Mukbang (먹방) refers to a Korean cultural export, having caught on in Korea and from there being spread beyond its borders. The word is a blend, deriving from the Korean words for 'eating' and 'broadcast' and thus also translates as 'eating show.' Basically, mukbang involve an individual who, while eating copious amounts of food, is engaging with their audience via talk in an online livestream. The origins of the genre can be found in Korea in the early 2010s and constitutive characteristics of the genre involve the amount and type of food consumed (which generally needs to be classifiable as excessive; most common food types include fast food and Korean dishes), the technical setup (i.e., livestreamed by a single camera with no editing), the participants (a single performer addressing a public audience of unspecified size), and ways of eating (namely, in an enjoyable way). In other words, mukbang performers have "to eat a lot, to eat fast, and to eat with relish" (Bruno & Chung, 2017: 159). Even though this might sound to some like a niche genre, it is important to keep in mind that popular mukbang streams and videos reach millions of views and famous mukbang performers earn their livelihood as internet celebrities. While mukbang have received abundant negative attention from the press due to their featuring of food excess and unhealthy eating behavior (picked up on in research in, e.g., social psychology; cf. Kang et al., 2020; Strand & Gustafsson, 2020), linguistic research has examined how mukbang create social cohesion and use language for the creation of joint eating actions. Choe (2019: 138), for instance, described how mukbang performers (also known as *broadcast jockeys*, *BJs*, or *mukbangers*) use recruitment strategies to create "act[s] of collaborative eating" and connect communication about food with eating food to enact digital commensality (Choe, 2021).

Mukbang, however, has not stayed confined to the Korean digital sphere. English-language mukbang have subsequently drawn the limelight, and instantiations of the genre can, in the meantime, be found around the globe. While the original Korean mukbang were largely livestreamed (with recordings at times uploaded later to video sharing platforms as a means to doubly monetize the material), the genre has evolved to span pre-recorded material (which was never livestreamed in the first place). This development went hand in hand with the inclusion of the word *mukbang* in the OED in 2021 (see Section 4). Research on asynchronous English-language mukbang produced in North America (and globally available on YouTube) has shown how performers design language use in the shows around notions of immediacy, informality, and intimacy to create social bonds with their viewers around a digital food experience (Rüdiger, 2020b, 2021c, 2022).

The English-language eating shows are thus a very successful development of the Korean mukbang genre, demonstrating how a genre as such can be exported and adapted to a different 'market.' In the following, we want to illustrate how English-language mukbang retain their cultural ties to the Korean context, though being produced in a different regional setting and a different language. Specifically, we draw on the eating show corpus collected by the first author (and used previously in Rüdiger, 2020b, 2021c, 2022), which consists of 100 English-language shows produced by ten performers for publication on YouTube and collected for research in 2018.[57] While a full analysis is beyond our scope here, we particularly focus on the video titles, giving additional examples from the transcripts of the videos to underline or extend the points made.

All shows in the corpus feature the term *mukbang* in their title with 19 percent additionally containing the term spelled in the Korean alphabet Hangul (i.e., 먹방), cf. (16) and (17).

(16)   The Sea of Cheese **Mukbang**
(17)   IN-N-OUT BURGER | **MUKBANG** [먹방]

This by itself already grounds the videos in the Korean mukbang tradition and sets viewer expectations. Other terms, such as *eating show* are also used but then in addition to the Korean term, see (18).

(18)   BIG FAT TACO BELL **MUKBANG**! (**Eating Show**)

Furthermore, the titles of the videos feature other references to the Korean context, such as Korean food items spelled in Korean (9 percent; see [19] for an example) and Korean food items spelled in English (5 percent; see [20]). The Korean origin of food is at times also simply specified with the adjective *Korean* (6 percent of videos in the dataset), as in (21).

(19)   SPICY RICE CAKE with CHEESE [떡볶이] | MUKBANG [먹방]
(20)   [mukbang/cookbang with THIEN]: Corn-Cheese **Kimchi** Fried Rice & **Bulgogi Ssam** (Pork Lettuce Wraps)
(21)   **KOREAN** FRIED CHICKEN + SPICY RICE CAKES MUKBANG! (Eating Show)

That viewers are not expected to be universally familiar with Korean foods can be seen, for instance, in (20), where *bulgogi ssam* is followed by an explanation in parenthesis ("Pork Lettuce Wraps"). Altogether, the video titles

---

[57] The videos were produced by seven female and three male performers, all of whom can be considered internet celebrities due to their production of eating shows. While some of the performers had a Korean diasporic background, this is not the case for most of them.

by themselves already implicate the Korean genre of mukbang, by including both explicit references to the genre itself and often evoking the Korean foodscape by references to specific dishes.

In addition, the set-up of the videos clearly makes them identifiable as mukbang (e.g., via the presentation of excessive amounts of food in front of the camera, the lack of different camera perspectives, etc.). In the videos themselves, we find 130 explicit references to *Korea* and *Korean* (distributed across 37 shows), and we do also come across code-switching beyond the names of dishes, for example, when phatically wishing viewers a good meal in Korean, singing Korean pop songs, or explaining Korean cultural concepts and idioms (cf. [22], [23], and [24]).

(22)   I know that in Korea you say like **soni keuda** so it basically means that when you're cooking something you make a lot like you make ten servings basically and there's only two people in the house

(23)   and this is known as **bapdoduk** in Korea which means rice thief because it's so yummy that you keep wanting to eat more and more rice

(24)   I think it's been a while uhm (claps) since I had the last uh Korean **Chuncheon Dakgalbi** that's uh **Chuncheon** is a city in Korea (text on screen reads: Chuncheon Dakgalbi spicy stir fried chicken, originated in Chuncheon) it started from **Chuncheon** in Korea or **Chuncheon Dakgalbi** that's why a lot of people when they open restaurants were like when you see in the menu it says **Chuncheon Dakgalbi** because they were uh you know it's kind of like Chicago pizza where it's where it started

Beyond vicarious pleasure, some of the videos thus spread knowledge about Korean food and culture, and the genre, particularly in its global, asynchronous format, plays an essential role in the entanglement of Korean and English both in the culinary (cf. the consumption of fast food items often strongly connected with the USA, such as hamburgers and fries vs. 'traditional' Korean dishes such as bulgogi mentioned earlier) and the linguistic sphere.

Conclusion

To summarize, we have discussed the global influence that Korea enjoys, if not commands, as part of its continuing cultural wave, seen in this section with a focus on K-pop and mukbang in particular. While entanglements of Korean and English language use are essential for both phenomena, this is decidedly more so the case in K-pop, where our study has shown a stellar rise of English use in the last fifteen years. Global eating shows ride the Korean wave by capitalizing on the popularity of mukbang, observable in the format of the genre but again also via linguistic means and cultural references. On an even more tangible level, the awareness of all things Korean is seen with, as one example, the proliferation of Korean goods establishments, such as *Oseyo*, which also sells Korean utensils and beauty products (e.g., face masks) in addition to many food items, often while K-pop videos and music can be seen and heard on a TV screen. Thus, a discussion of Korean Englishes is arguably incomplete without an inclusion of the ways in which Korean culture has spread globally, and the implications this has for the Korean language also being spread. K-pop, K-fashion, and K-food thus all contribute to the entanglements of Korean and English, further complicating an already complex language contact situation and, as a result, Korean Englishes emerge as a multi-contextual entity which can be realized in multiple ways.

6 Concluding Thoughts

In this Element, we surveyed and complicated the notion of 'transnational Korean Englishes' – by moving from the basic language contact situation between English and Korean in South Korea and the resultant linguistic forms (Section 2), to influences of English on Korean which demonstrate linguistic agency by language users (Section 3) and the corresponding opposite situation, the lexical influences that Korean has exercised on English as used around the globe (Section 4). Last but not least, we examined the role of hallyu – the K-wave – and how this plays out in K-pop and mukbang (Section 5). While all of these phenomena seem to be quite distinct from each other, we have claimed that they all form part of an interrelated transnational Korean Englishes complex as they are all traceable to the Korean-English contact situation. We have no doubt that research on transnational Korean Englishes will proliferate in the future – and as we have pointed out in each section, there is still very much that we do not know and remains to be investigated (and we list some suggestions for further research throughout this section).

Speaking of Korean English as a variety in the World Englishes sense, it can be a thorny issue to determine the point at which a linguistic variety can be said to have officially 'arrived' (see, e.g., Gut, 2011; Van Rooy, 2011; Baratta, 2019). This often reflects societal prejudice pertaining to notions regarding 'correct' and 'prestigious' forms of a given language. However, for the speakers of a language variety – here, Korean English – the language already has legitimization per the fact that they use it as such. Thus, rather than relying on 'traditional' methods of linguistic codification, such as school-based textbooks, prestigious dictionaries, and contexts reflecting societal power overall – such as education and government – we argue that the path to codification rests more than ever with the people who use the language. This is reflected, among others, in public signage, song lyrics, and social media, as demonstrated by the evidence that we presented in this manuscript. Corpus-based data has additionally provided ample evidence for the creative uses of Korean Englishes on the Korean peninsula and beyond. While the more traditional routes to codification, such as edited publications (Kruger & van Rooy, 2017) and dictionaries, certainly play a role, we should not ignore other indicators for variety status, including the lay dictionaries and glossaries investigated by Baratta (2021).

Terminology is certainly an important consideration in itself, and blended nomenclatures for World Englishes (such as *Konglish*) do not necessarily carry positive connotations (Baratta, 2019, 2021), while terms such as *English in Korea* downplay the creative uses of English found within Korean speaker communities (as attested throughout this manuscript). We appeal here to the responsibility of the research community in furthering the attention paid to 'unequal Englishes' (Tupas, 2015), that is, varieties that have received unduly little attention (with all the ideological and political repercussions that this brings with it) and to also reflect this in their terminological choices. We hope that the evidence presented in this manuscript contributes to and further encourages linguistic scholarship on Korean uses of English – not only restricted to the Korean peninsula because, as demonstrated in particular in Sections 4 and 5, it is used around the world. Korean and English entanglements are far-reaching and intricate, and certainly go beyond the use of English loanwords in Korean or the use of some lexical items by K-pop fans. While these phenomena certainly fall under the umbrella of 'transnational Korean Englishes' (as we proposed in this manuscript), we note that there are many other instantiations of the Korean English language complex which we were not able to discuss in the present text, such as Korean heritage communities around the globe (see, e.g., Kim, 2004), interviews of Korean celebrities in US-American talk shows, English-language Korean cookbooks, the use of Korean and English (as well as other languages potentially) at the US-American army bases in South Korea, and YouTube vlogs on Korean language and culture (as produced by Koreans but also, for instance, exchange students studying in Korea).

We are mindful of Edgar W. Schneider's (2004: 227) suggestion to "detect and trace . . . structural innovations as early as possible" and consider it therefore very desirable to expand on Korean English research to date (including what we presented in this Element) with historical approaches, such as the one presented by Rüdiger (in press) on the English textbooks used in Korea in the 1940s. Enhanced documentation of present-day Korean English features will also be helpful in tracing the ongoing developments within the variety. Ideally, this involves local and transnational uses of Korean English – as we have shown that looking at one also means looking at the other. It would, however, also be fruitful to consider how far subvariation has become a reality in Korean English, for example, if there are distinct registers of K-pop English, of Korean English newspaper writing, and such. Korean English has been put forward as a non-monolithic variety (Lee & Jenks, 2017), and finding features that vary across multiple contexts would provide further evidence for this. The linguistic implications for Korean English reflect what Pennycook (2007) refers to as transgression, in which the prefix *trans-* points to instances in which "the assumed boundaries between 'cultures' are reimagined and reconfigured through language" (Lee & Jenks, 2017: 8). Korean English, as a reflection of the varied uses of English by Koreans and non-Koreans alike (e.g., K-pop fans), can be understood as a plural, thus *Korean Englishes*. This involves potential subvarieties depending on genre (see Section 5 on the use of English in K-pop). Indeed, further studies are necessary, including those that involve wider samples of Koreans, differing abilities of English, and different age groups and professions. Let us dive more deeply into the world of transnational Korean Englishes and proclaim 'daebak' at its vitality and intricacy.

References

Ahn, H. (2014). Teachers' attitudes towards Korean English in South Korea. *World Englishes*, 33(2), 195–222. https://doi.org/10.1111/weng.12081.

Ahn, H. (2019). *Attitudes to World Englishes: Implications for Teaching English in South Korea*, London: Routledge. https://doi.org/10.4324/9781315394305.

Anthony, L. (2023). AntConc 2.4.2 [software]. www.laurenceanthony.net/software/antconc/.

Bamgbose, A. (1998). Torn between the norms? Innovations in World Englishes. *World Englishes*, 17(1), 1–14. https://doi.org/10.1111/1467-971X.00078.

Baratta, A. (2014). The use of English in Korean TV drama to signal a modern identity. *English Today*, 30(3), 54–60. https://doi.org/10.1017/S0266078414000297.

Baratta, A. (2019). *World Englishes in English Language Teaching*, London: Palgrave Macmillan. https://doi.org/10.1007/978-3-030-13286-6.

Baratta, A. (2021). *The Societal Codification of Korean English*, London: Bloomsbury.

Baratta, A. (2022). Stigmatised dictionaries housing a stigmatised variety of English: The use of Korean English online dictionaries as a teaching tool within the EFL classroom. *Lexikos*, 32(1), 250–271. https://doi.org/10.5788/32-1-1726.

BBC News (2018). BTS beat Harry Styles' Twitter record. www.bbc.com/news/entertainment-arts-45284261.

Bruno, A. L. & Chung, S. (2017). Mŏkpang: Pay me and I'll show you how much I can eat for your pleasure. *Journal of Japanese and Korean Cinema*, 9(2), 155–171. https://doi.org/10.1080/17564905.2017.1368150.

Buschfeld, S. (2013). *English in Cyprus or Cyprus English: An Empirical Investigation of Variety Status*, Amsterdam: John Benjamins. https://doi.org/10.1075/veaw.g46.

Buschfeld, S. & Kautzsch, A. (2017). Towards an integrated approach to postcolonial and non-postcolonial Englishes. *World Englishes*, 36(1), 104–126. https://doi.org/10.1111/weng.12203.

Chang, W., Park, Y., Kim, C. & Chang, D. (1989). *High School English I: Teacher's Guide*, Seoul: Donga Publishing.

Cho, J. (2012). Campus in English or campus in shock? Korean students hit hard by English-medium lectures. *English Today*, 28(2), 18–25. https://doi.org/10.1017/S026607841200020X.

Cho, J. (2017). *English Language Ideologies in Korea*: *Interpreting the Past and Present*, Cham: Springer. https://doi.org/10.1007/978-3-319-59018-9.

Cho, J. & Park, H.-K. (2006). A comparative analysis of Korean-English phonological structures and processes for pronunciation pedagogy in inter-pretation training. *Meta – Translators Journal*, 51(2), 229–246. https://doi.org/10.7202/013253ar.

Choe, H. (2019). Eating together multimodally: Collaborative eating in *mukbang*, a Korean livestream of eating. *Language in Society*, 48(2), 171–208. https://doi.org/10.1017/S0047404518001355.

Choe, H. (2021). Mukbang as your digital tablemate: Creating commensality online. In A. Tovares & C. Gordon, eds., *Identity and Ideology in Digital Food Discourse: Social Media Interactions Across Cultural Contexts*. London: Bloomsbury, pp. 137–167.

Choi, H. (2021). Anglicisms in Korean: A diachronic corpus-based study with special reference to translation as a mode of language contact. *Journal of Language and Linguistic Studies*, 17(1), 115–138.

Choi, L. (2021). 'English is always proportional to one's wealth': English, English language education, and social reproduction in South Korea. *Multilingua*, 40(1), 87–106. https://doi.org/10.1515/multi-2019-0031.

Darics, E. (2013). Non-verbal signalling in digital discourse: The case of letter repetition. *Discourse, Context & Media*, 2(3), 141–148. https://doi.org/10.1016/j.dcm.2013.07.002.

Davies, M. & Fuchs, R. (2015). Expanding horizons in the study of World Englishes with the 1.9 billion word Global Web-based English Corpus (GloWbE). *English World-Wide*, 36(1), 1–28. https://doi.org/10.1075/eww.36.1.01dav.

Duden. (n.d.). 'Kimchi.' www.duden.de/rechtschreibung/Kimchi.

Duffy, M. (2003). The subversion of Korean revisited? *English Today*, 19(3), 35–36. https://doi.org/10.1017/S0266078403003079.

Dunbar, J. (2023). Korea's 'K-Iceberg' continues to grow. *The Korea Times*. www.koreatimes.co.kr/www/nation/2024/04/113_344880.html.

Eaves, M. (2011). English, Chinglish or China English? *English Today*, 27(4), 64–70. https://doi.org/10.1017/S0266078411000563.

Education First. (n.d.). EF English Proficiency Index: South Korea. www.ef.com/wwen/epi/regions/asia/south-korea/.

Edwards, A. (2016). *English in the Netherlands*: *Functions, Forms and Attitudes*, Amsterdam: John Benjamins. https://doi.org/10.1075/veaw.g56.

Galloway, N. & Rose, H. (2015). *Introducing Global Englishes*, London: Routledge.

Gibson, J. (2020). How South Korean Pop Culture Can be a Source of Soft Power. In C. M. Lee & K. Botto, eds., *The Case for South Korean Soft Power*. Carnegie Endowment for International Peace. https://carnegieendowment .org/research/2020/12/the-case-for-south-korean-soft-power?lang=en.

GloWbE. (n.d.). Corpus of Global Web-Based English (GloWbE). www.eng lish-corpora.org/glowbe/.

GoWithGuide. (2024). Tourism in South Korea statistics 2023: All you need to know. https://gowithguide.com/blog/tourism-in-south-korea-statistics-2023-all-you-need-to-know-5254.

Gut, U. (2011). Studying structural innovation in new English varieties. In J. Mukherjee & M. Hundt, eds., *Exploring Second-Language Varieties of English and Learner Englishes*. Amsterdam: John Benjamins, pp. 101–124. https://doi.org/10.1075/scl.44.06gut.

Hadikin, G. (2014). *Korean English: A Corpus-Driven Study of a New English*, Amsterdam: John Benjamins. https://doi.org/10.1075/scl.62.

Hankyoreh. (2024). 2.5 million foreigners live in Korea, but little assistance is offered to the fast-growing segment. https://english.hani.co.kr/arti/english-edition/e_national/1130430.

Henry, E. S. (2010). Interpretations of 'Chinglish': Native speakers, language learners and the enregisterment of a stigmatized code. *Language in Society*, 39(5), 669–688. https://doi.org/10.1017/S0047404510000655.

Honna, N. (2006). East Asian Englishes. In B. Kachru, Y. Kachru & C. Nelson, eds., *The Handbook of World Englishes*. Hoboken, NJ: Blackwell Publishing, pp. 114–129.

HRDK. (n.d.). Human Resources Development Service of Korea: Overseas Employment Training Program (K-Move). www.hrdkorea.or.kr/ENG/5/2.

Jin, D. Y. & Ryoo, W. (2014). Critical interpretation of hybrid K-pop: The global-local paradigm of English mixing in lyrics. *Popular Music and Society*, 37(2), 113–131. https://doi.org/10.1080/03007766.2012.731721.

Jin, D. Y., Yoon, K. & Min, W. (2021). *Transnational Hallyu: The Globalization of Korean Digital and Popular Culture*, London: Rowman & Littlefield.

Jung, N. & Min, S. J. (1999). Some lexico-grammatical features of Korean English newspapers. *World Englishes*, 18(1), 23–37. https://doi.org/10.1111/1467-971X.00119.

Jung, S. K. & Norton, B. (2002). Language planning in Korea: The New Elementary English Program. In J. W. Tollefson, ed., *Language Policies in Education: Critical Issues*. Mahwah, NJ: Lawrence Erlbaum Associates, pp. 245–265.

Kachru, B. B. (1983). *The Indianization of English: The English Language in India*, Oxford: Oxford University Press.

Kachru, B. B. (1985). Standards, codification and sociolinguistic realism: The English language in the Outer Circle. In R. Quirk & H. Widdowson, eds., *English in the World: Teaching and Learning the Language and Literatures.* Cambridge: Cambridge University Press & The British Council, pp. 11–30.

Kang, H.-S. (2012). English-only instruction at Korean universities: Help or hindrance to higher learning? *English Today*, 28(1), 29–34. https://doi.org/ 10.1017/S0266078411000654.

Kang, S.-Y. (2017). US-based teacher education program for 'local' EIL teachers. In A. Matsuda, ed., *Preparing Teachers to Teach English as an International Language.* Bristol: Multilingual Matters, pp. 51–68. https://doi .org/10.21832/9781783097036-006.

Kang, E., Lee, J., Kim, K. H. & Yun, Y. H. (2020). The popularity of eating broadcast: Content analysis of "mukbang" YouTube videos, media coverage, and the health impact of "mukbang" on public. *Health Informatics Journal*, 26(3), 2237–2248. https://doi.org/10.1177/1460458220901360.

Kang, Y., Kenstowicz, M. & Ito, C. (2008). Hybrid loans: A study of English loanwords transmitted to Korean via Japanese. *Journal of East Asian Linguistics*, 17(4), 299–316. https://doi.org/10.1007/s10831-008-9029-5

Kelleher, S. (2024). South Korea is launching a visa just for K-pop fans. *Forbes*. www.forbes.com/sites/suzannerowankelleher/2024/01/02/south-korea-is-launching-a-visa-just-for-k-pop-fans/.

Kent, D. (1999). Speaking in tongues: Chinglish, Japlish and Konglish. *KOTESOL Proceedings of Pac 2*, 197–209.

Khedun-Burgoine, B. (2022). *"How do I make oppa sarang me?": Resemiotisation and reconstruction of meaning in the global Anglophone K-pop fandom.* Unpublished PhD thesis, Hertford College, University of Oxford.

Khedun-Burgoine, B. & Kiaer, J. (2023). *Korean Wave in World Englishes: The Linguistic Impact of Korea's Popular Culture*, New York: Routledge. https:// doi.org/10.4324/9780429200410.

Kiaer, J. (2021). *Delicious Words: East Asian Food Words in English*, London: Routledge. https://doi.org/10.4324/9780429321801.

Kim, E. (2020). A spread worthy of royalty. *New York Times*. www.nytimes .com/2020/09/28/dining/banchan-recipes.html.

Kim, E. G. (2011). English educational policies of the U.S. Army Military Government in Korea from 1945 to 1948 and their effects on the development of English language teaching in Korea. *Language Policy*, 10, 193–220. https://doi.org/10.1007/s10993-011-9204-9.

Kim, E. J. (2004). Korean-English bilinguals and heritage language maintenance. *The Korean Language in America*, 9, 244–258. https://doi .org/10.1075/sibil.32.13kim.

Kim, E.-Y. J. (2012). Creative adoption: Trends in Anglicisms in Korea. *English Today*, 28(2), 15–17. https://doi.org/10.1017/S0266078412000107.

Kim, E.-Y. J. (2021). 'King Sejong is crying': Korean people's perceptions of growing English usage in Korea. *English Today*, 37(3), 128–133. https://doi.org/10.1017/S0266078420000085.

Kim, E.-Y. J. (2022). A corpus-based study of anglicized neologisms in Korea: A diachronic approach to Korean and English word pairs. *International Journal of Corpus Linguistics*, 28(2), 125–143. https://doi.org/10.1075/ijcl.20055.kim.

Kim, M. (2015). The intelligence of fools: Reading the US Military Archive of the Korean War. *positions: east asia cultures critique*, 23(4), 695–728. https://doi.org/10.1215/10679847-3148382.

Kim, S. (2022). Blurring the boundaries: English–Korean bilingual creativity manifested in the linguistic landscape of South Korea. *English Today*, 38(2), 123–131. https://doi.org/10.1017/S0266078420000474.

Kim, S. (2024). 'Ehh? Order through kiosk? What's that?' Public attitudes towards the excessive Anglicisation of commerce in South Korea. *Journal of Multilingual and Multicultural Development*, 45(6), 1922–1937. https://doi.org/10.1080/01434632.2022.2033247.

Kim S.-H. & Lee, H. (2023). Asserting Koreanness in South Korean middle school English textbooks. *World Englishes*, 42, 544–561. https://doi.org/10.1111/weng.12548.

Korea Foundation. (n.d.). www.kf.or.kr/kf/main.do.

Korean Film Council. (n.d.). Box Office Yearly. www.koreanfilm.or.kr/eng/news/boxOffice_Yearly.jsp?mode=BOXOFFICE_YEAR&selectDt=2023&category=ALL&country=ALL.

Kortmann, B., Lunkenheimer, K. & Ehret, K. (eds.) (2020). The Electronic World Atlas of Varieties of English. https://ewave-atlas.org/.

Kruger, H. & van Rooy, B. (2017). Editorial practice and the progressive in Black South African English. *World Englishes*, 36(1), 20–41. https://doi.org/10.1111/weng.12202.

Lawrence, C. B. (2010). The verbal art of borrowing: Analysis of English borrowing in Korean pop songs. *Asian Englishes*, 13(2), 42–63. https://doi.org/10.1080/13488678.2010.10801282.

Lawrence, C. B. (2012). The Korean English linguistic landscape. *World Englishes*, 31(1), 70–92. https://doi.org/10.1111/j.1467-971X.2011.01741.x.

Lee, C. (2021). Hidden ideologies in elite English education in South Korea. *Journal of Multilingual and Multicultural Development*, 42(3), 221–233. https://doi.org/10.1080/01434632.2020.1865383.

Lee, C. G. & How, S.-M. (2021). Hallyu tourism: Impacts on inbound tourists to South Korea. *Current Issues in Tourism*, 25(9), 1361–1367. https://doi.org/10.1080/13683500.2021.1924637.

Lee, J. S. (2004). Linguistic hybridization in K-pop: Discourse of self-assertion and resistance. *World Englishes*, 23(3), 429–450. https://doi.org/10.1111/j.0883-2919.2004.00367.x.

Lee, J. S (2006). Linguistic constructions of modernity: English mixing in Korean television commercials. *Language in Society*, 35(1), 59–91. https://doi.org/10.1017/S00474045060600390.

Lee, J. S. (2007). *I'm the illest fucka*: An analysis of African American English in South Korean hip hop. *English Today*, 23(2), 54–60. https://doi.org/10.1017/S026607840700209X.

Lee, J. S. (2011a). Globalization and language education: English village in South Korea. 어학연구, 47(1), 123–149.

Lee, J. S. (2011b). Globalization of African American vernacular English in popular culture: *Blinglish* in Korean hip hop. *English World-Wide*, 32(1), 1–23. https://doi.org/10.1075/eww.32.1.01lee.

Lee, J. S. (2012). *Please Teach Me English*: English and metalinguistic discourse in South Korean film. In J. S. Lee & A. Moody, eds., *English in Asian Popular Culture*. Hong Kong: Hong Kong University Press, pp. 127–149.

Lee, J. S. (2013). Hybridizing medialect and entertaining TV: Changing Korean reality. In R. Rubdy & L. Alsagoff, eds., *The Global-Local Interface and Hybridity: Exploring Language and Identity*. Bristol: Multilingual Matters, pp. 170–188. https://doi.org/10.21832/9781783090860-011.

Lee, J. S. (2014). English on Korean television. *World Englishes*, 33(1), 33–49. https://doi.org/10.1111/weng.12052.

Lee, J. S. (2016). 'Everywhere you go, you see English!' Elderly women's perspectives on globalization and English. *Critical Inquiry in Language Studies*, 14(4), 319–350. https://doi.org/10.1080/15427587.2016.1190654.

Lee, J. S. (2020). English in Korea. In K. Bolton, W. Botha & A. Kirkpatrick, eds., *The Handbook of Asian Englishes*. Hoboken, NJ: Wiley-Blackwell, pp. 585–604.

Lee, H. J. & Jin, D. Y. (2019). *K-Pop Idols: Popular Culture and the Emergence of the Korean Music Industry*, London: Lexington Books.

Lee, J. W. & Jenks, C. J. (2017). Mapping Korean Englishes in transnational contexts. In C. J. Jenks & J. W. Lee, eds., *Korean Englishes in Transnational Contexts*. London: Palgrave Macmillan, pp. 1–19. https://doi.org/10.1007/978-3-319-59788-1_1.

Lee, K. (2008). Mapping out the cultural politics of 'the Korean Wave' in contemporary South Korea. In B. H. Chua & K. Iwabuchi, eds., *East Asian*

Pop Culture: *Analyzing the Korean Wave*. Hong Kong: Hong Kong University Press, pp. 175–189. https://doi.org/10.5790/hongkong/9789622098923.003.0010.

Lee, S. (1989). The subversion of Korean. *English Today*, 5(4), 34–37. https://doi.org/10.1017/S0266078400004338.

Lee, S. & Nornes, A. M. (eds.) (2015). *Hallyu 2.0*: *The Korean Wave in the Age of Social Media*, Ann Arbor: University of Michigan Press. https://doi.org/10.3998/mpub.7651262.

Lee, S. H. (1986). *Language change in Korean with special emphasis on semantic change of English loanwords*. Dissertation, University of Cologne.

Lee, S. H. (2019). 'I am still close to my child': Middle-class Korean wild geese fathers' responsible and intimate fatherhood in a transnational context. *Journal of Ethnic and Migration Studies*, 47(9), 2161–2178. https://doi.org/10.1080/1369183X.2019.1573662.

Lee, S. H. (2021). *Korean Wild Geese Families*, Lanham, MD: Lexington Books.

Leuckert, S. & Rüdiger, S. (2020). Non-canonical syntax in an Expanding Circle variety: Fronting in spoken Korean(ized) English. *English World-Wide*, 41(1), 33–58. https://doi.org/10.1075/eww.00039.leu.

Li, D. (2010). When does an unconventional form become an innovation? In A. Kirkpatrick, ed., *The Routledge Handbook of World Englishes*. London: Routledge, pp. 617–633.

Li, D. C. S. & He, D. (2021). When does an unconventional form become an innovation? In A. Kirkpatrick, ed., *The Routledge Handbook of World Englishes*, 2nd edition. London: Routledge, pp. 617–633.

Locher, M. A. (2020). Moments of relational work in English fan translations of Korean TV drama. *Journal of Pragmatics*, 170, 139–155. https://doi.org/10.1016/j.pragma.2020.08.002.

Marinescu, V. (ed.) (2014). *The Global Impact of South Korean Popular Culture*: *Hallyu Unbound*, London: Lexington Books.

Mair, V. (2023). Taylor Swift fanilect. https://languagelog.ldc.upenn.edu/nll/?p=57890.

Meriläinen, L. (2017). The progressive form in Learner Englishes: Examining variation across corpora. *World Englishes*, 36(4), 760–783. https://doi.org/10.1111/weng.12244.

Mesthrie, R. & Bhatt, R. M. (2008). *World Englishes: The Study of New Linguistic Varieties*, Cambridge: Cambridge University Press. https://doi.org/10.1017/CBO9780511791321.

Miley, S. (2023). Sustaining the economic miracle: South Korea to break global top ten by 2026. *The Centre for Business and Economics Research*. https://

cebr.com/reports/sustaining-the-economic-miracle-south-korea-to-break-glo bal-top-ten-by-2026/.

Moody, A. & Matsumoto, Y. (2012). Lu-go and the role of English loanwords in Japanese: The making of a 'pop pidgin.' In J. S. Lee & A. Moody, eds., *English in Asian Popular Culture*. Hong Kong: Hong Kong University Press, pp. 103–126.

Morin, N. (2019). K-Pop 101: The terms you need to know before you stan. www.refinery29.com/en-us/k-pop-music-fans-terms-meaning.

Morrett, H. (2011). *Korean ESL students' use of English definite articles*. Unpublished thesis of the honors program, Liberty University, Lynchburg, VA: USA.

Moskin, J. (2015). Maangchi: YouTube's Korean Julia Child. *New York Times*. www.nytimes.com/2015/06/03/dining/maangchi-youtube-korean-julia-child.html.

Mufwene, S. (2001). *The Ecology of Language Evolution*, Cambridge: Cambridge University Press. https://doi.org/10.1017/CBO9780511612862.

Nahm, A. (1993). *Introduction to Korean History and Culture*, Carlsbad, CA: Hollym.

Nam, J. Y. & Southard, B. (1994). Orthographic representation and resyllabification of English loan words in Korean. *Language and Speech*, 37(3), 259–281. https://doi.org/10.1177/002383099403700304.

NOW. (n.d.). NOW Corpus (News on the Web). www.english-corpora.org/now/

Nye, J. (2004). *Soft Power*, New York: Public Affairs.

OED. (n.d.). 'fighting.' www.oed.com/dictionary/fighting_int?tab=meaning_ and_use.

OED. (n.d.). 'K- combining form.' www.oed.com/dictionary/k_combform?tab= meaning_and_use.

OED. (n.d.). 'kimchi.' www.oed.com/dictionary/kimchi_n?tab=meaning_ and_use.

OED. (n.d.). 'Konglish.' www.oed.com/dictionary/konglish_n?tab= meaning_and_use.

OED. (n.d.). 'manicure.' www.oed.com/dictionary/manicure_n?tab=meaning_ and_use.

OED. (n.d.). 'meeting.' www.oed.com/dictionary/meeting_n?tab= meaning_and_use.

OED. (n.d.). 'oppa.' https://www.oed.com/dictionary/oppa_n?tab=meaning_ and_use.

OED. (n.d.). 'skinship.' www.oed.com/dictionary/skinship_n?tab= meaning_and_use.

OED. (n.d.). 'trot.' www.oed.com/dictionary/trot_n4?tab=meaning_and_use.

Oh, Y. & Son, H. (2024). Lexical borrowing in Korean: A diachronic approach based on a corpus analysis. *Corpus Linguistics and Linguistic Theory*, 20(2), 407–431. https://doi.org/10.1515/cllt-2022-0102.

Park, J.-H. (2024). S. Koreans' average TOEIC score ranks 16th. *The Korea Herald*. May 27, 2024. www.koreaherald.com/view.php?ud=20240527050527.

Park, J.-K. (2009). 'English fever' in South Korea: Its history and symptoms. *English Today*, 25(1), 50–57. https://doi.org/10.1017/S026607840900008X.

Park, J. S.-Y. (2003). 'Baby, Darling, Honey!' Constructing a competence of English in South Korean TV shows. *Texas Linguistic Forum*, 47, 143–154.

Park, J. S.-Y. (2009). *The Local Construction of a Global Language: Ideologies of English in South Korea*, Boston: De Gruyter Mouton. https://doi.org/10.1515/9783110214079.

Park, J. S.-Y. (2010). Images of 'good English' in the Korean conservative press: Three processes of interdiscursivity. *Pragmatics and Society*, 1(2), 189–208. https://doi.org/10.1075/ps.1.2.01par.

Park, J. S.-Y. (2013). English, class and neoliberalism in South Korea. In L. Wee, L. Lim & B. H. Goh, eds., *The Politics of English*: *South Asia, Southeast Asia and the Asia Pacific*. Amsterdam: John Benjamins, pp. 287–302. https://doi.org/10.1075/wlp.4.19park.

Park, J. S.-Y. (2021). Konglish as cultural practice: Reconsidering the English language in South Korea. *International Journal of TESOL Studies*, 3(3), 138–152. https://doi.org/10.46451/ijts.2021.10.05.

Park, S. J. & Abelmann, N. (2004). Class and cosmopolitan striving: Mothers' management of English education in South Korea. *Anthropology Quarterly*, 77(4), 645–672. https://doi.org/10.1353/anq.2004.0063.

Park, S.-Y. & Kang, Y.-Y. (2024). Private education spending in S.Korea hits new record high. *The Korea Economic Daily*, March 15, 2024. www.kedglobal.com/economy/newsView/ked202403150009.

Pellant, G. (2023). The UK's largest Asian supermarket chain is coming to Manchester Arndale. *The Manc*, July 26, 2023. https://themanc.com/news/uks-largest-asian-supermarket-chain-oseyo-manchester-arndale.

Pennycook, A. (2007). *Global Englishes and Transcultural Flows*, London: Routledge. https://doi.org/10.4324/9780203088807.

Percillier, M. (2016). *World Englishes and Second Language Acquisition*: *Insights from Southeast Asian Englishes*, Amsterdam: John Benjamins. https://doi.org/10.1075/veaw.g58.

Petrosyan, A. (2024). Languages most frequently used for web content as of January 2024, by share of websites. *Statista*. www.statista.com/statistics/262946/most-common-languages-on-the-internet/.

Pham, J. (2020). 25 K-pop fandom words every K-pop stan should know. *StyleCaster.* https://stylecaster.com/feature/k-pop-fandom-words-1153522/.

Qiang, N. & Wolff, M. (2003). The Chinglish syndrome: Do recent developments endanger the language policy of China? *English Today,* 19(4), 30–35. https://doi.org/10.1017/S026607840300405X.

Richelle. (2016). Learning the KPOP language. *Amino.* https://aminoapps.com/c/k-pop/page/blog/learning-the-kpop-language/YkIb_ueZPGaMMBzXdMp m1LJbVZrw2z.

Rosen, A. (2016). The fate of linguistic innovations: Jersey English and French learner English compared. *International Journal of Learner Corpus Research,* 2(2), 302–322. https://doi.org/10.1075/ijlcr.2.2.08ros.

Rüdiger, S. (2014). The nativization of English in the Korean context: Uncharted territory for World Englishes. *English Today,* 30(4), 11–14. https://doi.org/10.1017/S0266078414000340.

Rüdiger, S. (2016). Cuppa coffee? Challenges and opportunities of compiling a conversational English corpus in an Expanding Circle setting. In H. Christ, D. Klenovšak, L. Sönning & V. Werner, eds., *A Blend of MaLT: Selected Contributions from the Methods and Linguistic Theories Symposium 2015.* Bamberg: University of Bamberg Press, pp. 49–71.

Rüdiger, S. (2018). Mixed feelings: Attitudes towards English loanwords and their use in South Korea. *Open Linguistics,* 4(1), 184–198. https://doi.org/10.1515/opli-2018-0010.

Rüdiger, S. (2019). *Morpho-Syntactic Patterns in Spoken Korean English,* Amsterdam: John Benjamins. https://doi.org/10.1075/veaw.g62.

Rüdiger, S. (2020a). English in South Korea: Applying the EIF model. In S. Buschfeld & A. Kautzsch, eds., *Modelling World Englishes: A Joint Approach to Postcolonial and Non-Postcolonial Varieties.* Edinburgh: Edinburgh University Press, pp. 154–178.

Rüdiger, S. (2020b). Dinner for one: The use of language in eating shows on YouTube. In S. Rüdiger & S. Mühleisen, eds., *Talking About Food: The Social and the Global in Eating Communities.* Amsterdam: John Benjamins, pp. 145–165. https://doi.org/10.1075/impact.47.08rud.

Rüdiger, S. (2021a). Non-postcolonial Englishes in East Asia: Focus on Korean popular music. In B. Schneider & T. Heyd, eds., *World Englishes – Volume 1: Paradigms.* London: Bloomsbury, pp. 207–223. https://doi.org/10.5040/9781350065833.0021.

Rüdiger, S. (2021b). The use of *like* in Korean English speech. *World Englishes,* 40(4), 548–561. https://doi.org/10.1111/weng.12540.

Rüdiger, S. (2021c). Digital food talk: Blurring immediacy and distance in YouTube eating shows. *Anglistik*, 32(2), 111–130. https://doi.org/10.33675/ANGL/2021/2/9.

Rüdiger, S. (2022). Intimate consumptions: YouTube eating shows and the performance of informality. *Internet Pragmatics*, 5(1), 115–142. https://doi.org/10.1075/ip.00070.rud.

Rüdiger, S. (in press). English in Korea. In R. Hickey, ed., *New Cambridge History of the English Language*. Cambridge: Cambridge University Press.

Rüdiger, S., Leuckert, S. & Leimgruber, J. R. E. (eds.) (in press). *World Englishes and Social Media*: *Platforms, Variation, and Meta-Discourse*, London: Bloomsbury.

Salazar, D. (n.d.). Daebak! The OED gets a K-update. www.oed.com/discover/daebak-a-k-update/.

Scherling, J. (2012). *Japanizing English*: *Anglicisms and Their Impact on Japanese*, Tübingen: Narr Verlag.

Schneider, E. W. (2003). The dynamics of New Englishes: From identity construction to dialect birth. *Language*, 79(2), 233–281. https://doi.org/10.1353/lan.2003.0136.

Schneider, E. W. (2004). How to trace structural nativization: Particle verbs in World Englishes. *World Englishes*, 23(2), 227–249. https://doi.org/10.1111/j.0883-2919.2004.00348.x.

Schneider, E. W. (2007). *Postcolonial English*: *Varieties Around the World*, Cambridge: Cambridge University Press. https://doi.org/10.1017/CBO9780511618901.

Schneider, E. W. (2014). New reflections on the evolutionary dynamics of World Englishes. *World Englishes*, 33(1), 9–32. https://doi.org/10.1111/weng.12069.

Shim, R. J. (1999). Codified Korean English: Process, characteristics and consequence. *World Englishes*, 18(2), 247–258. https://doi.org/10.1111/1467-971X.00137.

Sohn, H.-M. (1999). *The Korean Language*, Cambridge: Cambridge University Press.

Sohn, H.-M. (2006). Korean in contact with Chinese. In H.-M. Sohn, ed., *Korean Language in Culture and Society*. Honolulu: University of Hawai'i Press, pp. 44–56.

Song, J. J. (2012). South Korea: Language policy and planning in the making. *Current Issues in Language Planning*, 13(1), 1–68. https://doi.org/10.1080/14664208.2012.650322.

Sprague, J. (2024). Doenjang in the air: *Maangchi* and the mediation of Korean cultural authenticity. *Humanities*, 13(1), 5, n.p. https://doi.org/10.3390/h13010005.

Statista. (2024). Number of inbound visitors to South Korea from 2000 to 2023. www.statista.com/statistics/709116/south-korea-inbound-visitors/.

Story of Mandy. (2010). Konglish. https://minniehwang.wordpress.com/2010/05/23/konglish/.

Strand, M. & Gustafsson, S. A. (2020). Mukbang and disordered eating: A netnographic analysis of online eating broadcasts. *Culture, Medicine, and Psychiatry*, 44, 586–609. https://doi.org/10.1007/s11013-020-09674-6.

Takeshita, Y. (2010). East Asian Englishes: Japan and Korea. In A. Kirkpatrick, ed., *The Routledge Handbook of World Englishes*. London: Routledge, pp. 265–281.

Tan, S. X.-W. & Tan, Y.-Y. (2015). Examining the functions and identities associated with English and Korean in South Korea: A linguistic landscape study. *Asian Englishes*, 17(1), 59–79. https://doi.org/10.1080/13488678.2015.999406.

Thorkleson, T. S. (2005). Konglish in the classroom: The teachers' backdoor. Presented at KOTESOL, Daegu workshop on June 4, 2005.

Touhami, B. & Al-Abed Al-Haq, F. (2017). The influence of the Korean wave on the language of international fans: Case study of Algerian fans. *Sino-US English Teaching*, 14(10), 598–626. https://www.davidpublisher.com/index.php/Home/Article/index?id=34487.html.

Tranter, N. (1997). Hybrid Anglo-Japanese loans in Korean. *Linguistics*, 35, 133–166. https://doi.org/10.1515/ling.1997.35.1.133.

Tupas, R. (ed.) (2015). *Unequal Englishes: The Politics of Englishes Today*, Basingstoke: Palgrave Macmillan. https://doi.org/10.1057/9781137461223.

Tyson, R. (1993). English loanwords in Korean: Patterns of borrowing and semantic change. *El Two Talk*, 1(1), 29–36.

van Rooy, B. (2011). A principled distinction between errors and conventionalized innovation in African Englishes. In J. Mukherjee & M. Hundt, eds., *Exploring Second-Language Varieties of English and Learner Englishes: Bridging a Paradigm Gap*. Amsterdam: John Benjamins, pp. 189–207. https://doi.org/10.1075/scl.44.10roo.

Wikipedia. (n.d.). 'BTS.' https://en.wikipedia.org/wiki/BTS.

Wikipedia. (n.d.). 'Music Bank (TV Program).' https://en.wikipedia.org/wiki/Music_Bank_(TV_program).

Yeon, J. & Brown, L. (2011). *Korean: A Comprehensive Grammar*, London: Routledge. https://doi.org/10.4324/9780203833001.

Cambridge Elements $\equiv$

World Englishes

Edgar W. Schneider
University of Regensburg

Edgar W. Schneider is Professor Emeritus of English Linguistics at the University of Regensburg, Germany. His many books include *Postcolonial English* (Cambridge, 2007), *English around the World, 2e* (Cambridge, 2020) and *The Cambridge Handbook of World Englishes* (Cambridge, 2020).

About the Series
Over the last centuries, the English language has spread all over the globe due to a multitude of factors including colonization and globalization. In investigating these phenomena, the vibrant linguistic sub-discipline of "World Englishes" has grown substantially, developing appropriate theoretical frameworks and considering applied issues. This Elements series will cover all the topics of the discipline in an accessible fashion and will be supplemented by on-line material.

Cambridge Elements ≡

World Englishes

Printed in the United States
by Baker & Taylor Publisher Services